Gerontius and Other Poems

by

Pete Gage

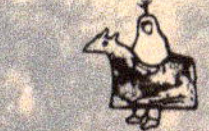

THE HOBNOB PRESS

2022

First published in the United Kingdom in 2022

by The Hobnob Press,
8 Lock Warehouse, Severn Road, Gloucester GL1 2GA
www.hobnobpress.co.uk

British Library Cataloguing in Publication Data
A catalogue record for this book is available from the British Library

ISBN 978-1-914407-31-4

Typeset in Adobe Garamond Pro 14/17 pt.
Typesetting and origination by John Chandler

In memory of my friend
John Hills
who passed away on
12th January 2022

Glastonbury, Somerset

1 Some Time

Some time, sometimes I feel,
I'll feel the truth,
the very real man within me as I go.
But then, when ideals are worn to nil,
I see I'll never need
to value such as will be truth.
No; truth will be,
and have as right,
its right to have, and be,
the essense of it all… life.
As beauty has its truth,
so these insights
will seem more pure;
so too will life contain this truth,
and all shall be this once,
just once,
this once for all time,
truth.

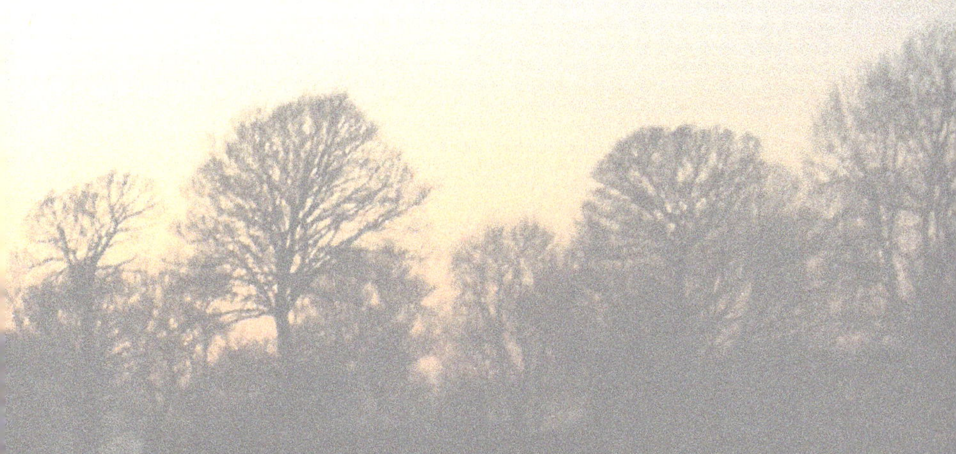

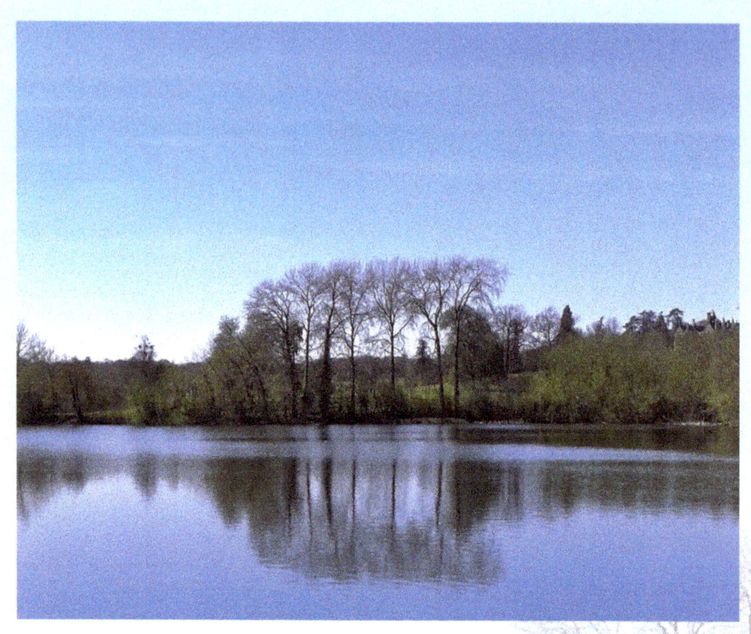

Orchardleigh Estate, Near Frome, Somerset

2 There's a Spirit that Lives Close to Me

There's a spirit that lives close to me,
as close as even skin to me,
still nearer to my bone.
It sails within my bloodstream,
it is peace inside my brain.
It whispers in my lungs to me;
and pacifies my pain.

This spirit living here inside,
will murmur in my heart.
It is speech within my mouth to me,
and metal in my muscle.
It rides above my hopelessness,
obliterates my doubt;
feels for me and breathes in me;
it turns my demons out.

O spirit living close to me,
refine this, my integrity;
be passive when I'm angry,
be freedom in my liberty.
O spirit, ever timeless,
be my fluid, and my food;
be the birth in my mortality,
anticipate my mood.

Cable Bay, Anglesey , Wales

3 My Dancer

There, by marker, goes my dancer.
Where we whirl, wherever fancied,
that is round the tips of freedom,
up and down a fiery floor.
there at rest inside my castle,
that is where we took the night.
all along the banks we danced
until we reached the open sea.

Sliding down the crumbling rockface
of the wispy cliffs of time,
past a thousand other demons:
those who once had held us there.
Once, when first we turned our backs
upon perfection and its captains,
once when we were tangled, willing
to surrender and to die.

Now across the bays of heaven,
resting in the light of days;
now, with bodies to the salt-spray,
all is pure that once was foul.
Sprinkled, soft and speckled beauty
cleanly pierces every pore;
clears again, as once when we were
young it did, our simple souls.

Now we lie in another castle,
resting in the evening starshine
from our day of lovers dancing,
made by us for freedom's glow.
We are full, with juices flowing;
on the crest of wilder dreams,
filled with life, as now beneath us,
fading slowly, black clouds die.

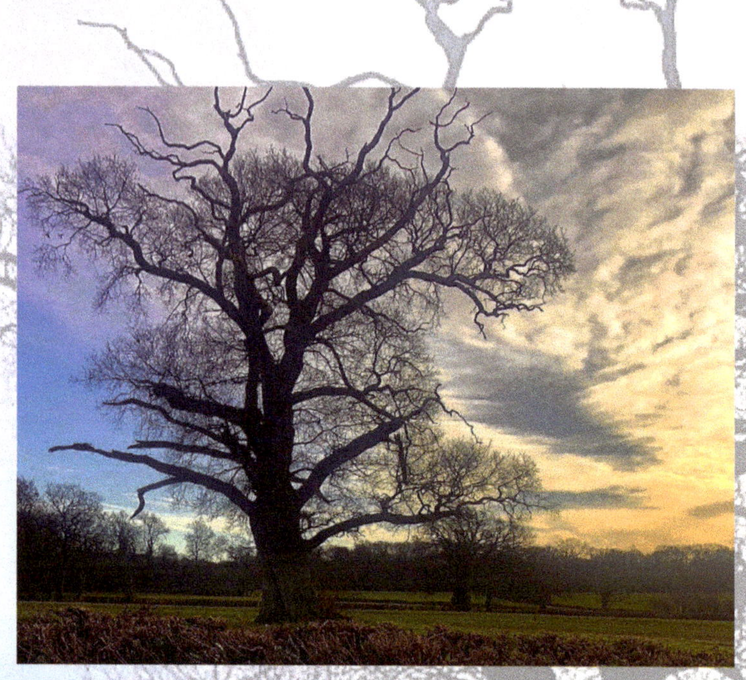

Berkley, Near Frome, Somerset

4 Gerontius – Part One

In quiet gardens, Gerontius,
this song will rise slowly to your soul;
the pools of your silence will bathe you
in the warm night of your death.
Bidding the moment bring forth the dawn,
you'll feel the gentle trickle
of a life dissolving through the haze,
sacred and profound as the harp in dance

in the early moments of your new day.
No wild imaginings will stir,
but easing through the cool air,
mellowing in the blinking of an eye,
a still fragment of eternity will appear.
In the corners of your new world,
its mild heart turned to an open sky,
your natural song will rise to your heaven,
as a bird in a timeless flight.
The gift of your death will stir,
its songbird claiming your willing soul,
flight and flower merging in grand crescendo,
creating their vision, bright as a gypsy's dance.
Choruses from the shimmering light will race
in a torrent round the sun all the dancing day,
the ringing tambourine of the heart
resounding through the fountains of your song.
All will celebrate your pleasure in it,
rejoicing as at the turn of each season.
And in the fiery moment of this intoxication,
laughter in the furnace of the soul,
the scorching minute of ecstasy
will smoulder on the devil's floor.

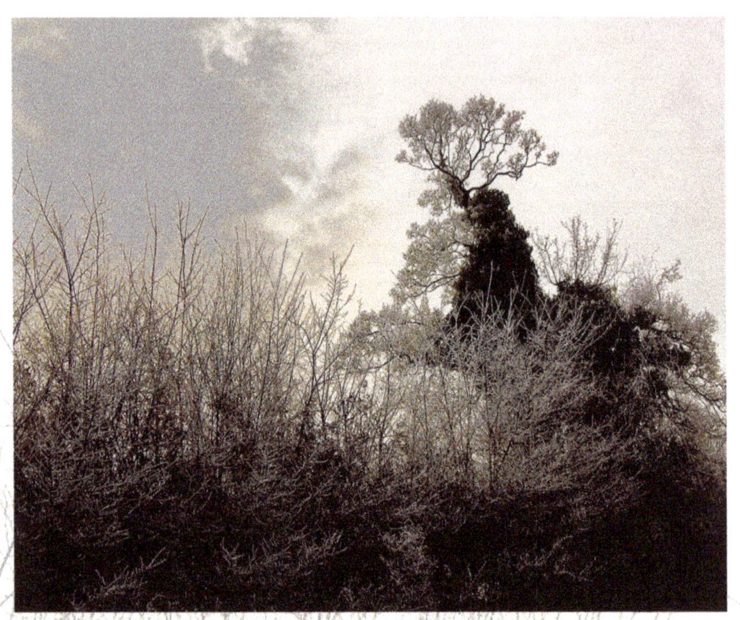

Cuckoo Lane, Frome, Somerset

5 Winter

Into your swelling bosom with the cold,
when the bark is icy-crisp above your root;
into your darkest seasons' thrown-off chasms,
those who called you "home" now crawl;
into the icy fire of your heart they leap,
in vain hope they'll reach the centre of your flame;
into your open mouth the frost holds hard and tight;
their brittle lips leave all too much alone.

The song they sang for seasons now fades
on the crest of their resistant ride.
You, from whose face they turn
when first their land is drained of warmth,
have taken breath enough at last
to chill the softest air with a song
only murmured as you stir.
As sharp as your blade is long,
again you burst upon the land
on frozen paths they run.

No truth for those in heaven or the mind's hell;
only winter, when they followed like flies
to the cave, or the comfort of the puppy's kennel.
What little thought for that which now they invade,
a land now opening the door
in the weakest wisp of hope
that truth has knocked.

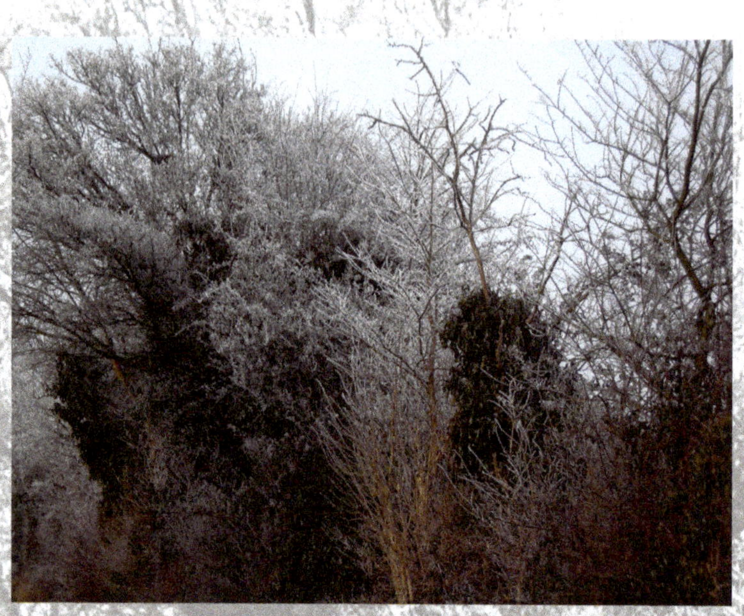

Cuckoo Lane, Frome Somerset

6 Infinity

Into finite and final prisms, light,
on simple journeys through the fire, cracks,
splinters soft on a chosen brink
and fades beyond eternity's path.
Our reason flickers, half as deep
as did the crazy light first pierce.
Our journey though has found its truth
in the sanctitude of infinity.
Why then, why, that light whose mirrors dull
with each new prismic corner turned,
why does she give insight into
death behind the wall?

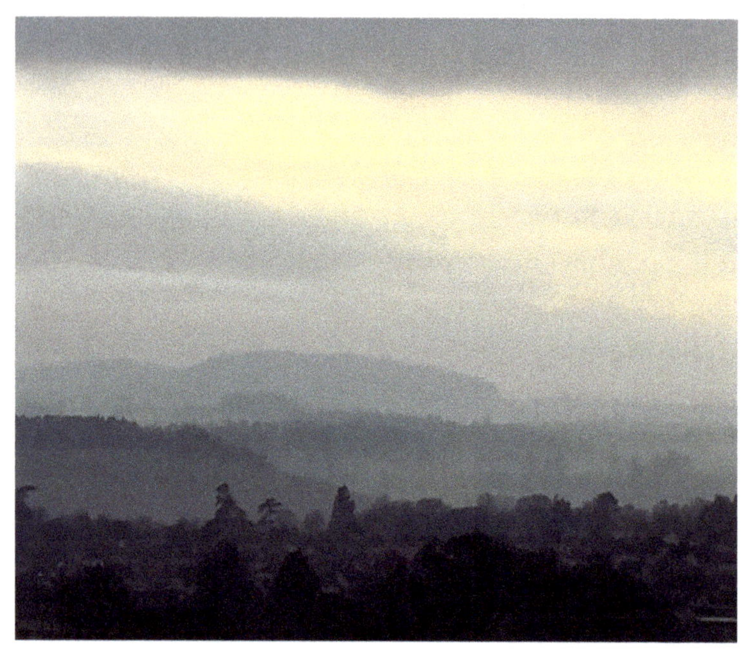

View from Cley Hill, Near Warminster, Wiltshire

7 Peace, Land!

Peace, land!
You mother your people,
silently caressing the undetermined soul.
You free the grasping enemy
who prances off in spite of sin,
the food psychotic thought
had cooked too well.

Peace, land!
You offer all I said you stole.
Handfuls of you lapping over your brim;
peace too much for this dry, empty cup.
With what modesty you brush away the tears
from pores, still trickling from their aching eyes!
What precious consolation for their wrinkled brow.

Peace at last within;
the sea-bed whole
of that rugged yelping storm
is silent now the curves of your waves are smooth.

Peace, land!
You offer peace to me.
Your breath gives warmth to soothe
the splitting, chapping tongue.
You offer me that once taken.
Now it's mine again to give.

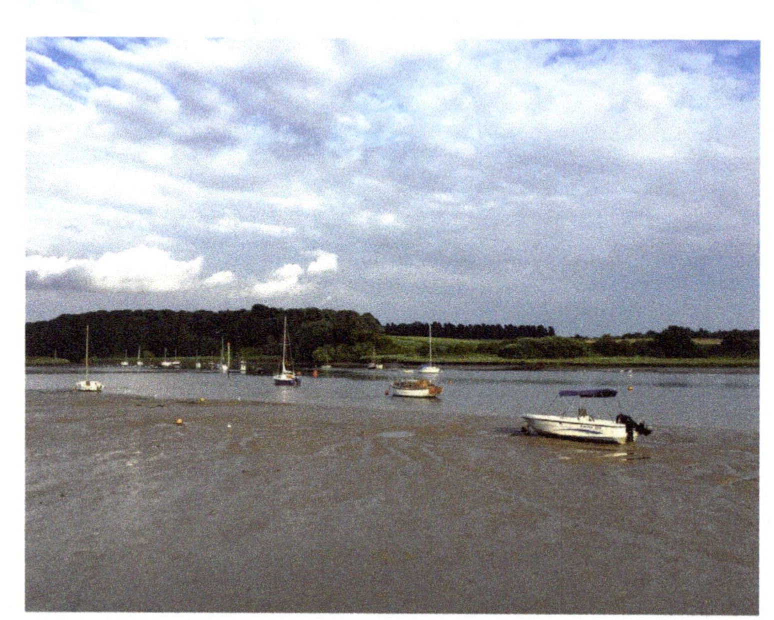

Orford, Near Woodbridge, Suffolk

8 Gaverne Evening

There lies, still, and o, at last,
lasting the fathoms' features,
curling pathways, hid,
deep inside the mouths of rocks
where chanting war-cries split the drums,
a cove so grand that mountains fail
to grasp such portly grandeur.
A red sun blinks
behind the lids of clouds;
a half-hid, drowsy, skulking sun
inspires our one last gasping breath.
What unknowing depths
we have travelled.
We lag unseen
beneath the end of the day
and fall beside the pleasant silence
on our first day's rest.
Gaverne, now with pious soul
that rises over all its woven tapestries,
has given, gives, its massive sigh.
Eyes, these eyes; others of the land;
silent others, child, my child,
my others, reap this joy!
The evening sings its simple song;
o ears, my ears, I hear.

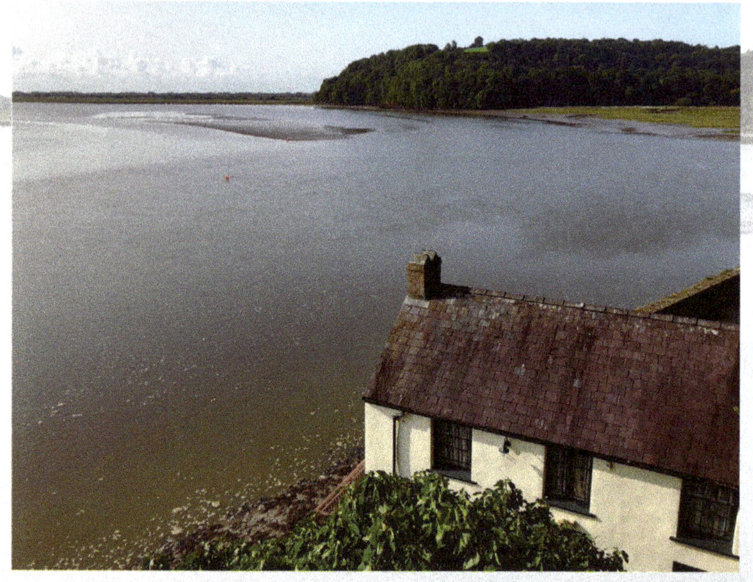

Boat House (Dylan Thomas's Home), Laugharne, Carmarthenshire, Wales

9 Silence

Silence, pure silence;
silence, without the memory of sound.

Peace, perfect peace;
listened to, though unperceived.

Light, absolute light;
light, without the memory of shade.

White, sheer white;
observed, though unnoticed.

Stillness, dead stillness;
stillness, without the memory of movement.

Calm, statuesque calm;
untouched, though deeply felt.

A gentle serenity;
singing, yet tuneless;
echoing, but not resounding.
A subdued radiance;
coloring, yet toneless;
shining, but not enlightening.
A fertile desolation;
quivering, yet motionless;
vibrating, but not disturbing.

Time immeasurable;
an infinite void;
constant clarity;
sustained simplicity.

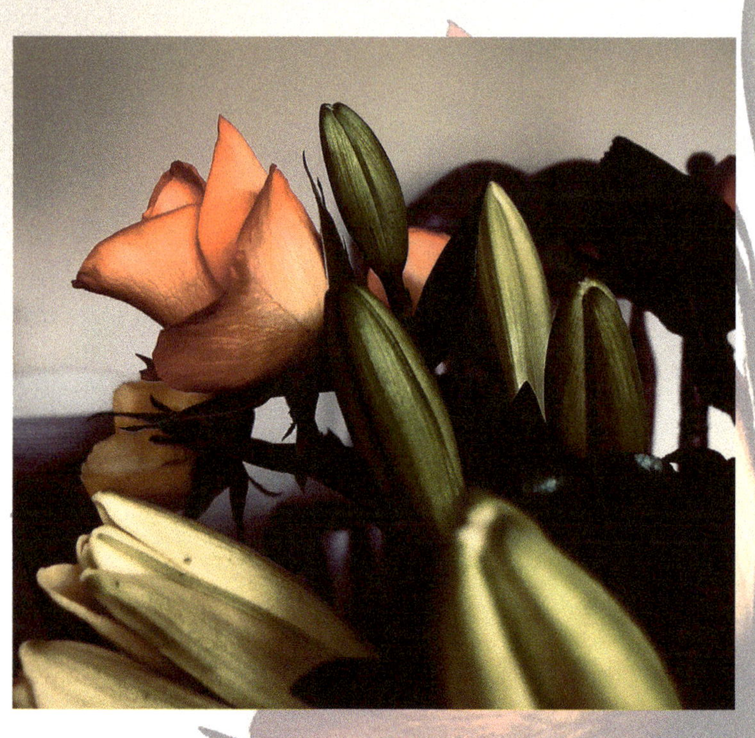

Frome, Somerset

10 Sonnet

If I were man, and man enough to try.
From this my heart I'd let a songbird say
The most of which a man could only cry,
The half of which I mutter through the day.
But though I am a man, no tears I shed,
Except for when my weaknesses are bare;
So I shall keep my song inside my head
And tell another story, should I dare,
About another songbird I have seen:
A singing bird whose song I can't dismiss;
A bird who has and sometimes hasn't been
The meaning for a tantalising kiss.
    And I shall let the song within my heart
    Be kept for you my love while we're apart.

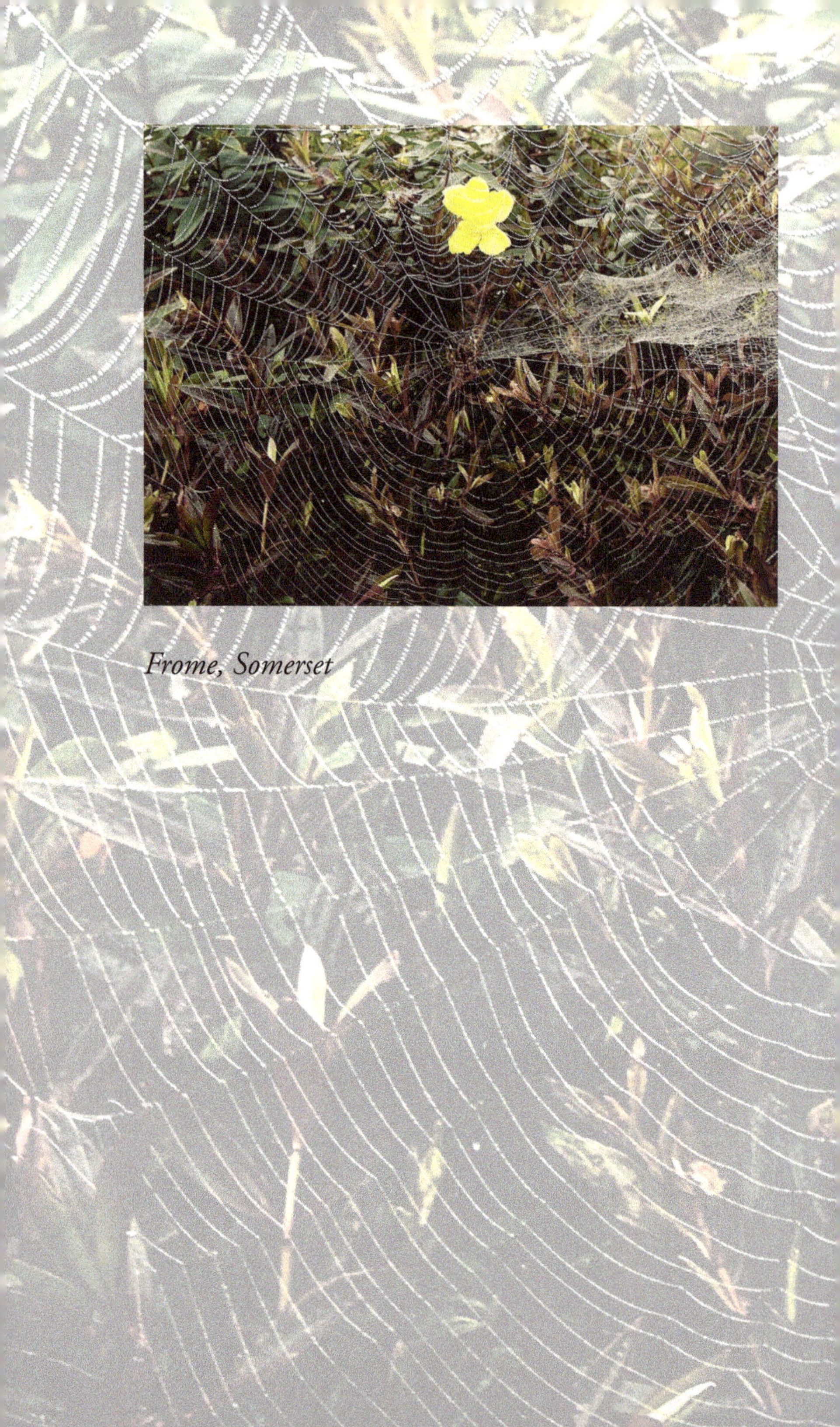

Frome, Somerset

11 Gerontius – Part Two

Beware the howling gales of Hades,
lest the black storm of conflict
rips through your flesh,
tearing at your heart in the night,
and goaded by the demons of your childhood,
turning on a whim to ruffle your sleeping head,
creasing the brow, and knifing the spirit
with the ache of a hurricane piercing;
ferocious challenges of the body pushed aside;
the cutting salt-wind whipping the face of serenity;
and the fiery tempest spitting at the cringing muscle,
your desperate breath tormented in the backlash;
pounded by uncertainty, blood from the soul,
anger in the artery, all crippling the limb;
confused moments of half-truths
hanging on the twisted branches.
Now stand with the knife held high, white knuckled,
bare-hearted, and raging at the years of despair.

View from Cley Hill, Near Warminster, Wiltshire

12 Would You?

If I stood on a hill
and gave praise to the clouds,
would you picture me there on the mound,
silhouetted against
the drama of my universe?

If I were to stir,
would you be true to me,
my song a new one
that before, you did not know?

Would you strip away
the sentiment,
so it's the heart and not the ego
that will beat and bellow
its own most intimate secrets?

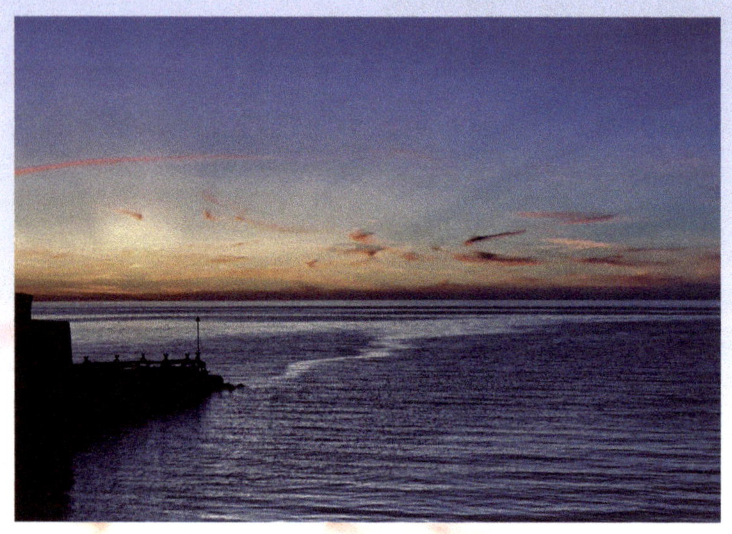

Aberaeron, Ceredigion, Wales

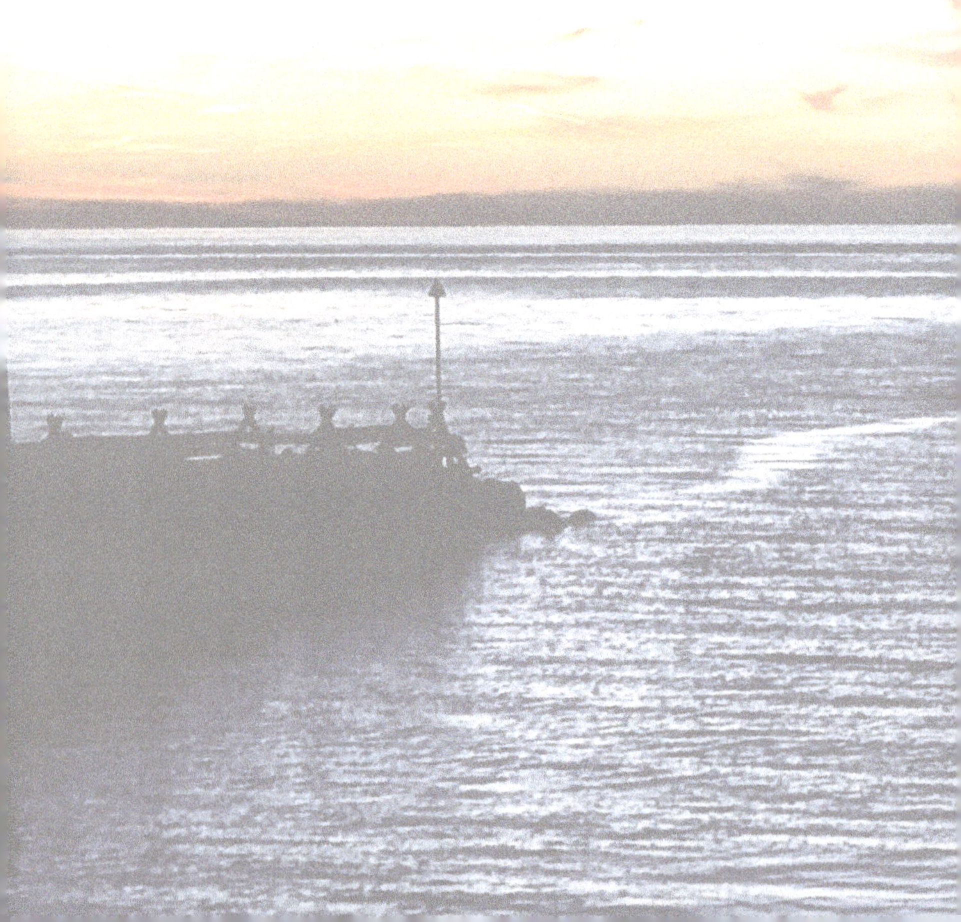

13 Then You Appeared

Then you appeared,
bursting through the air in your nervousness,
out of that drab old school house with the smell of
paint;
this, your home, where later we'd cling to each other
on a single bed; learning to take it slow,
as we fought to deny our most passionate needs.
Your high-street jumper and flared jeans
were as blue as the July sky;
your wavy hair fell around your young clear face,
and your eyes determined not to falter or embrace
this clutch of campus heroes distracted by your
innocence.
This was the first of my many stirrings,
your body so tidily framed and acceptable.
I remember a craving for your attractive normality,
though I'd never have told you at the time;
my reasoning thrived on my past dependencies,
memories of mood or grandiose youthful ideas
that would elevate the sunken treasure of my fading
childhood.
I never considered your reality to be a choice.

We moved like lovers into summer and found it was
fitting.
I've never forgotten that concentrated look you wore
that disguised your womanly worth.

Under-estimating your freedom
to choose what was right for you,
I denied you credit for your most creative choices.
Still, you conjured for me a simple epitome,
protected and protecting a precious anonymity,
that, if mine, would engulf me I fear,
dissolving the security of my self-made persona.
Your modest ambition, your regular background,
seduced me and threatened me.
You were hidden in the pack, unproud,
with straight-forward philoosphies,
undefined by a screaming intellect;
they lured me from my manic ramblings,
artful aspirations and pretentious imitations,
and all those fantastic images for my desperate soul.
Your innocence was the lifebelt you threw
as I choked on the choppy waters of my tormented
    fortune.
I had found a subtle temptress
whose decisions were reared in camouflaged recesses;
whose facial expressions denied me all access
to your private emotions.
So I invented them for you, and foisted them on
    you,
insisting you take what you never had needed.

I thought you a canvas upon which my picture
would evolve to my liking, refusing you entry,
(deluded deception!!) inventing my female

upon your unsuspecting background.
Still undetected, your stifled truth simmered,
neglected as I fed you my addiction
to my lifestyle inventions.
My waves swallowed your identity,
tossed aside your simplicity
as we two drifted into lost oceans, uncharted
territory,
our ship's captain, this mad dictator
drunk at the wheel on a sea of fear.
We built our picture of life
like two unsupervised children;
childhood sweethearts mingling with the adults,
with grown-up toys and real money,
sometimes even setting their style.
If they doubted me, I'd cut them down with vocal
ease,
fuelling my anger with their beer and wine.
I fully believed they were seeing my point,
unaware of their despairing of me,
blind to their leaving me behind,
and insensitive to your loyalty at my side.
I thought that we were practising at life,
but this was the real thing!
We lived within a capsule that I casually steered,
to go with any wind that took my fancy.

You looked on, internalising your dismay,
as we sped to ever-changing destinies,

sailing on my fears through time,
our feet hardly touching the ground.
You ached beneath the rubble of our existence,
nurturing our only two reasons for being:
the love you reserved for our two daughters.
You rose from the chaos as nature intended;
and your patience snapped when reality insisted;
you burst through the door of our drab house
with its smell of loss and confusion,
to watch your plants take root again
as they sucked at the earth beneath our feet,
unsteadying the rotting soil,
and churning the turning worm.
This was your internal sunrise,
the male and female of your very own growth,
the beginning of your existance
in the steady glasshouse of your independence.
I banged like a madman on your door
while you abandoned all fear inside.
It would be years till you showed me
your innocent face again;
I'd surrendered to your unaffected simplicity.
as you quietly wore your modest stability
beneath velvet and cotton from India;
flowing behind you, patchouli identity,
the acceptable face of your gypsy fantasy.
I watched you forge your winning ways,
anchored to our shipwreck chains;
you stood unflinching from the ravages of our

journey,
disguising your shattered esteem in dance.
You had bled from all sides, never asking for mercy,
rendering my aching-to-care for you useless,
and severing my life-source connection to your
sanity,
in your last ditch bid to help me survive.
When your silence unnerved me, I hungered to be
repaired.
We had been witness to our own desolation;
we watched from our deserted perches,
waiting like vultures to salvage the spoils.

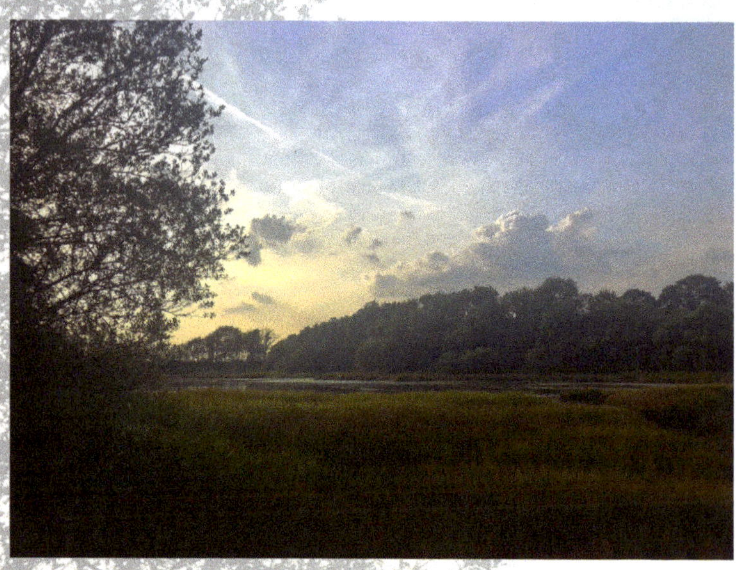

View From Pond Cottage, Landshipping, South Pembrokeshire, Wales

14 What Light Is Threatening?

What light is threatening
this restless shadow?
Not the glow of a shining talent,
expressive painter, poet describing;
not even the precious jewel, reflecting
radiance upon inventions born,
desired and seized at every turn.
Shadows tend to cower, recoil,
beside this light penetrating the void,
and illuminating the deepest well.

This blinding light, rightly shone,
dissolves the murky medium,
shatters our granite despair
to dust, afloat on its purest ray.
This, the light of the unborn,
unhindered by man's dalliance;
never to lie, revealing a visionless truth.

Darkness comes over the late afternoon,
but its warmth waits on in the shadows.
The birds sing, undisturbed,
while leaves of copper dance
at the whim of the breeze.
In all weathers, I disappear,
amongst new arrivals
into the invisible air.

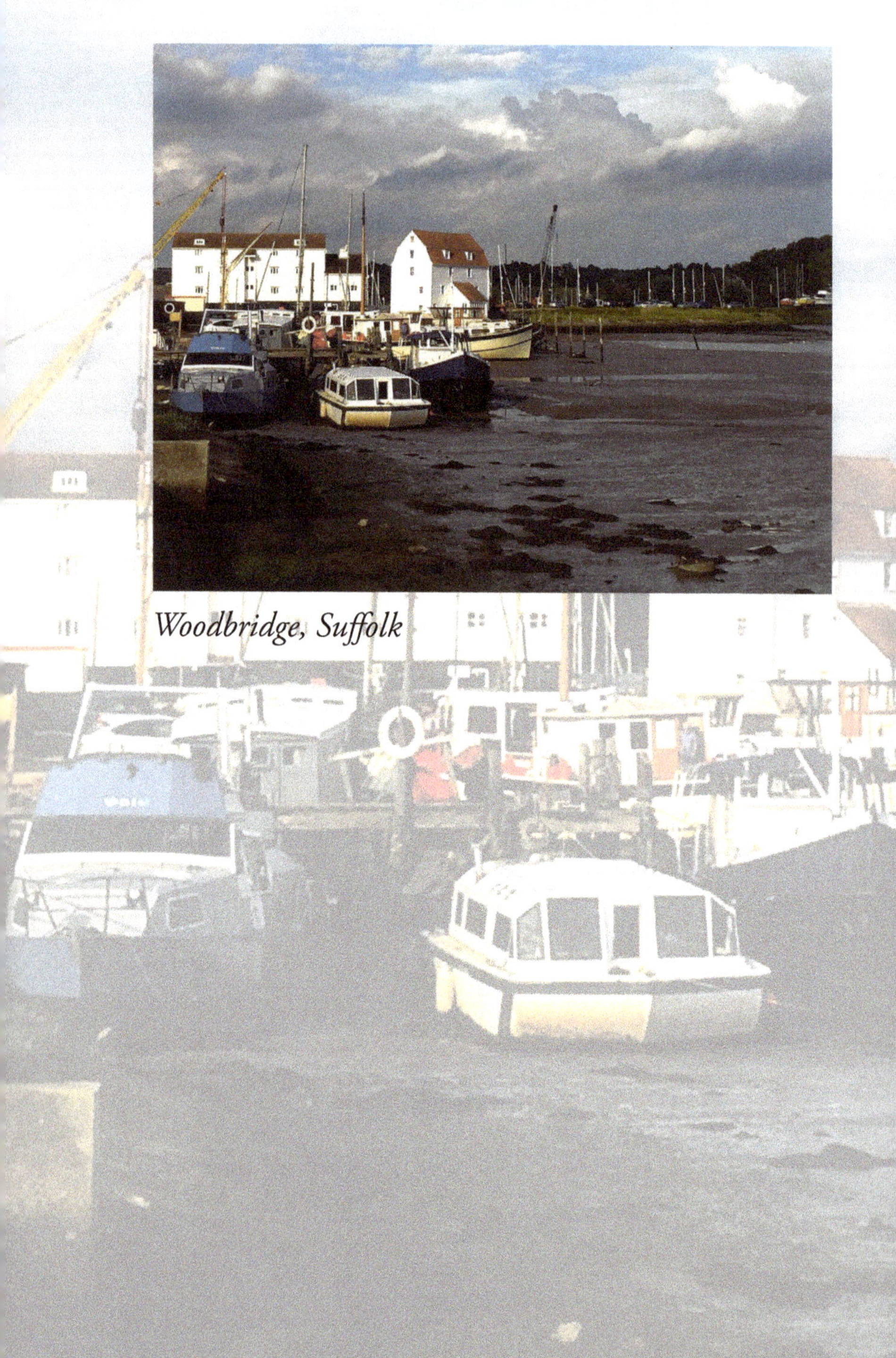

Woodbridge, Suffolk

15 Spirit Lives On in the Flesh

Silence in the hollow of my heart,
The flame is low;
the vapour rises from the gut:
carried on the wind of life-giving breath
through the channels of my pathways,
lifted again, face to the sun,
to melt among the branches of fruitless trees,
unwanted by hungry ghosts,
unnoticed and undone,
the rapid patterns of thought fading
against the hazy backdrop of an empty mind.

I'm here in the saviour's garden,
where the night never mocks me,
and shadows of memory
lurk in its darkest corners.
There's no mystery, nor adventure,
nor romance in the heaving silence.
Spirit wandered through my head
like a child without a mother,
searching without consciousness,
removed from all communion,
those flames still flickering.
I hold on to life with shallow sighs,
like the breath of a sleepng dog.
Spirit lives on in my flesh.

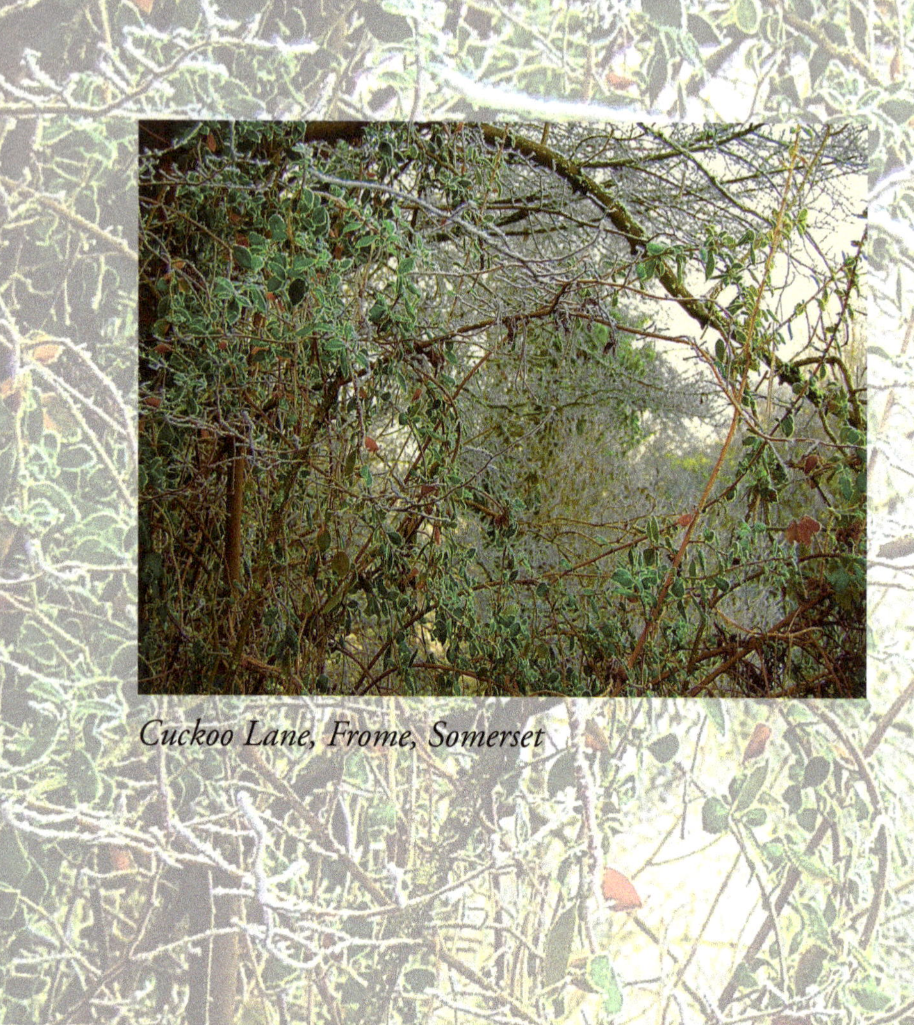

Cuckoo Lane, Frome, Somerset

16 Death Will Not Absolve Us

Death will not absolve us;
nor will the dead forgive.
They will penetrate the cracks in our fibre.
Our rituals will go unnoticed
and we will pay for our misdemeanours.
They will sting the sinews,
and scorch the metal of our soul.
And though we beg them for their silence,
their screams will pierce our membranes,
our waters dissolving the tissue of our lies.
They won't send us a warning;
but they'll take us down
with their burning fragments,
slow and unforgiving.
This will be our living hell:
life torn from our limbs.
leaving only that which we despaired of.
They will offer no pity;
neither to our brothers nor our sisters.
They'll learn we faked compassion,
and cursed them while they lived;
that we judged them as they died;
this will be our epitaph
earned in our blind communion
with the living Lucifer.
We will be swallowed up in their mystery.
And no-one will ever tell us
what they know.

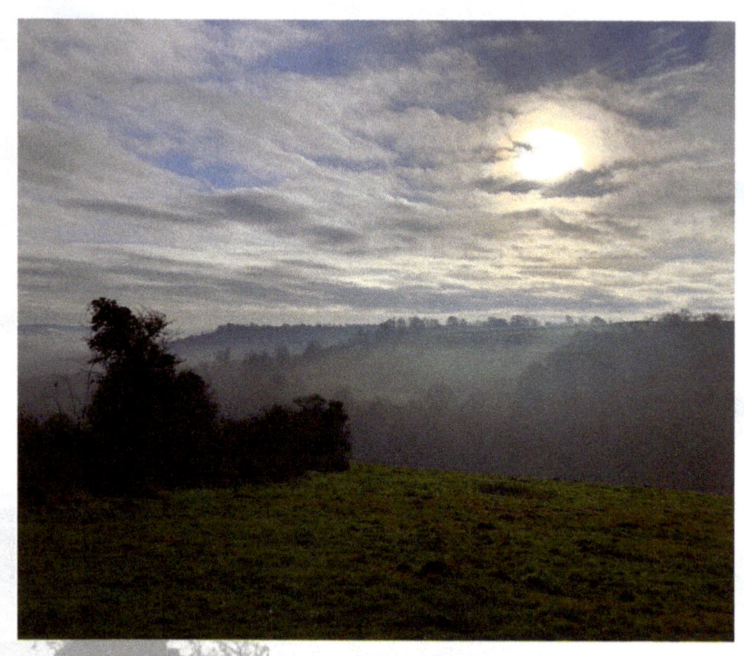

Charlcombe, Near Lansdown, Bath

17 Your Rights and Your Concessions

Your rights and your concessions
have been scattered to the wind.
You who have journeyed
in defeat and degradation,
console your own weary eagle,
desolate on those rocky crevices;
the sorry cries of your most wicked heart
can surrender to your protagonists.
The poet and the painter will lie silent;
they'll leave the stage shattered,
confused and in despair.
All you floundering wretches;
curses on your sanctimonious ravings.
Now is the time for your subservience.
I will salvage what was left to me,
and create from your apologies,
a new home, to sit in my cold serenity,
presiding over judges and their juries.
I will weep no more for my neglected child;
I'll watch over him like a wolf.
I'll take the crown from you
and offer it to the beggar in my heart.
My eyes will not bear a trace of a tear,
and your sorrowful procession
will pass my door no more.

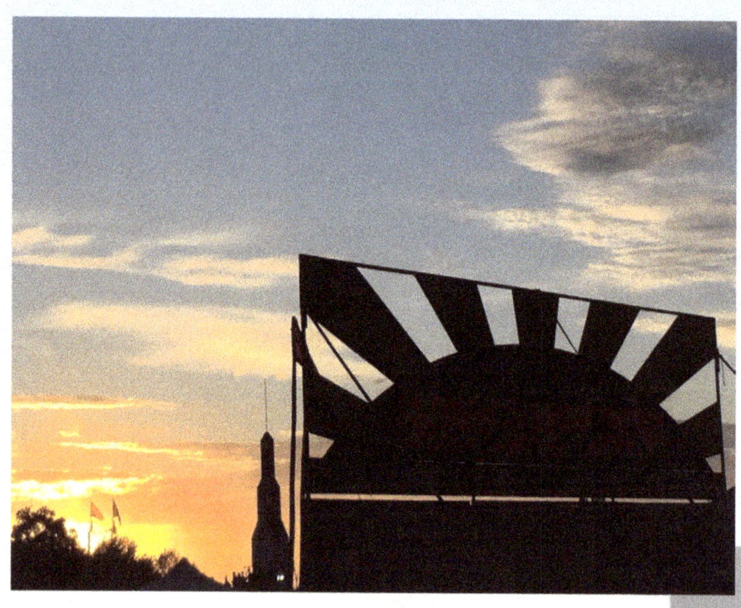

Glastonbury Festival, Somerset

18 Fractured Wing

You glide past me now like a hurried swan,
eyes straight ahead, quest ever-changing,
shape of your heart once bloated by a lively pulse,
now shrunken by ice-cool blood.
Some shape of heart persuades you to believe;
to shelter from whatever is the truth.

You in your mantle,
woven from the spoils of our war,
hiding a conspiracy;
silence nourished by withheld promises.

Sever the life-line, breath of life remaining,
long-since expelled,
faded hopes of part-time lovers,
whims that gave you reason,
justifying each moment,
along your lifeline.

You sail on by with a fractured wing,
held steady 'til you're gone,
your proud head turns to reveal
only the corner of your eye.

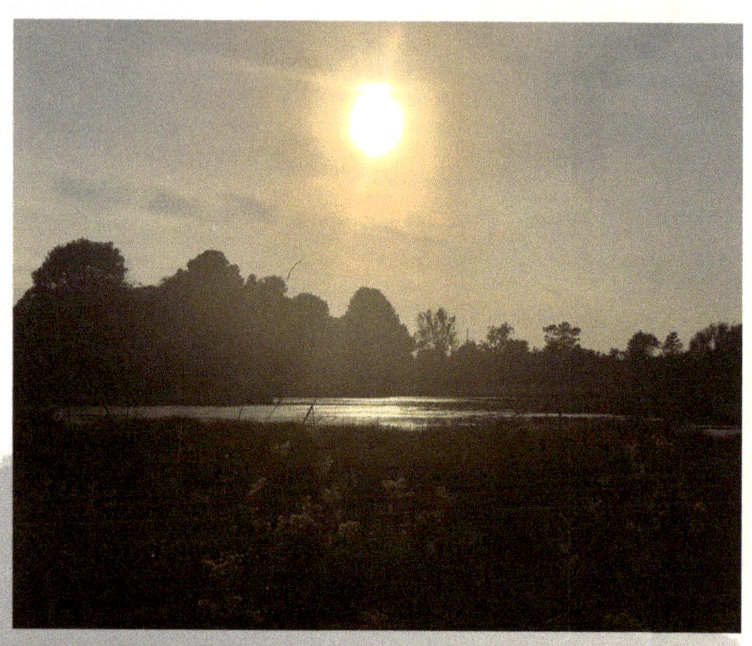

View from Pond Cottage, Landshipping, South Pembrokeshire, Wales

19 Poem to an Unborn Child

Murmur child, if only to the silence you respond.
And as you leave those walls wherein you lie,
warm your mother with gentle breath.
Enter, you, spirit of child we are yet to know;
face your mortal, she;
suckle, body wet from nest you left behind;
catch the eyes of she who bears her soul for you;
opens herself up for you who promises to arrive.
And in the pleasure of your suckling,
taste the tears the willing mother sheds for you;
be the one you were with her
before the cord was severed;
trust those heavenly arms of hers,
cocooned as now you are,
that one day you may also know
as I today have known in she:
that paradise is held in the first breath you take:
the murmur of your exquisite birth.

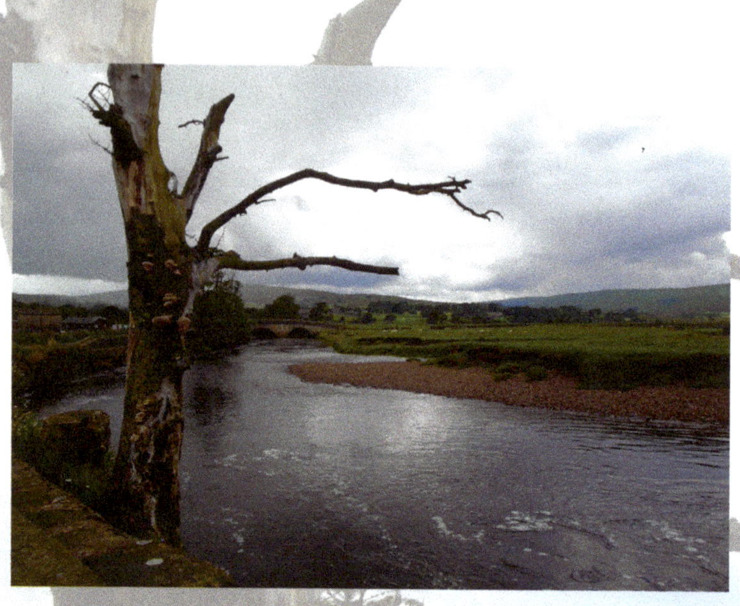

Near Hawes, Wensleydale, North Yorkshire

20 It's Time to Go Back

It's time to go back away from here,
where sleepless dreams enfold me in their warm fantasy;
away from this heady mix of two intrepid souls.
It's time to return to the relentless river,
where the days are dark and long
away from here where the clear waters flow
like spirits in the night, and our hearts are soft and light.
Lead us back to focus on the life we lived before.
Back, yes, from what our hearts can hardly bear to lose;
to the soft and grassy verge on which we lay,
our dance so full of flair, the dizzy heights so rarified;
so clean the sea-soaked air.

Take us back for fear that we may falter,
here on the precipice of reason;
back to the place we knew long ago;
with its drawn-out nights of dreamless sleep;
our feet on a recognised road,
safe as houses, and secure away from here.
Take us back to our blissful home
of passions blown and strewn about as petals
we trod as if in heaven.
For it was love we found in the heart of our kinship.
Now is the time to go back,
lest we're smothered in the arms of complacency,
or lost in delusions of security.
Take us back again to the abyss
and leave us as you often did,
to fend for our own survival,
still unbroken, and not alone.
It's time to go back, before these fears
engulf us in the sorrow of our parting;
for we have touched the core of love;
don't let it slip through our fingers like the sand.
Take us back with cold awakening
before our ending has burned away our bliss.

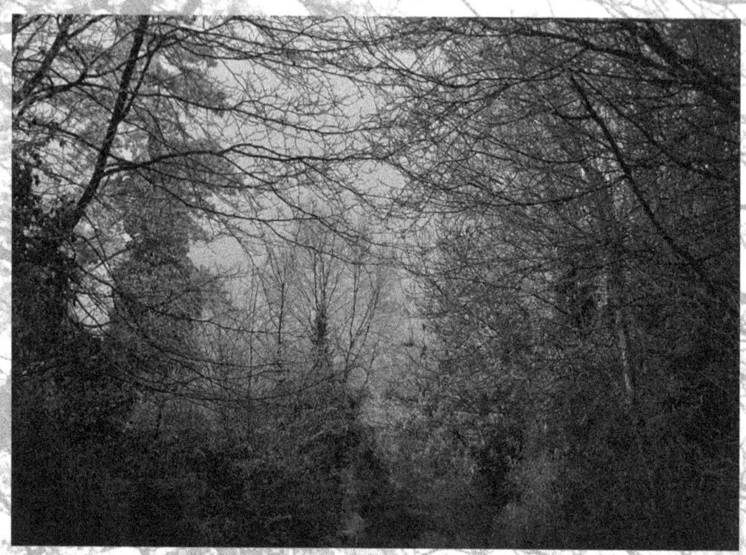

Cuckoo Lane, Frome, Somerset

21 Gerontius – Part Three

Your sweet sighs of recognition will rise
from the empty soil of your grey evening;
dusk, this doleful hour, twilight at your gate,
mellow moments melting on the ground,
and the wail of your anguish
withering in the misty silence.
A crumbling notion of experience
turns to sand, vast unspoken messages
of the looming night, embracing
the bare bones of your dark and woody statue.
The universal worship of nobility sounds,
riding on the wings of stony angels,

the fallen evening at their feet,
and leaving the soul to pass through your flesh.
Willing to surrender, your spirit is a flaking sinew,
in the soil and in the season,
bringing closeness to the night,
perfume for the living and the dead.
There's nowhere so acceptable as here in the mother-heart;
enveloped with the warm thrust of your tender age,
not yearning for mercy, nor molecule of measured beauty,
nor instinct in the fallen hour.
You return to the womb, all your loves meandering,
dry upon the soil, now flowering in the shade of your barren night.
They break out of their loneliness,
the screams of youth muted by this local death,
while you prepare for the gaping days of your own weaknesses.
You are the willing participant in the solemn march to ecstasy,
pressed as a flower in the lost eternities of youth,
drawing on sonorities that burn through your symphonies,
rhythms bursting through the dances of your scherzos.
Your masculine wealth revealed in the ultimate agreement.
All entries valid in the eternal moment. sliding into rapture,
as forgotten mirrors crack on disused floors,
memories only whispering advantages,
predictions only looking back in time.

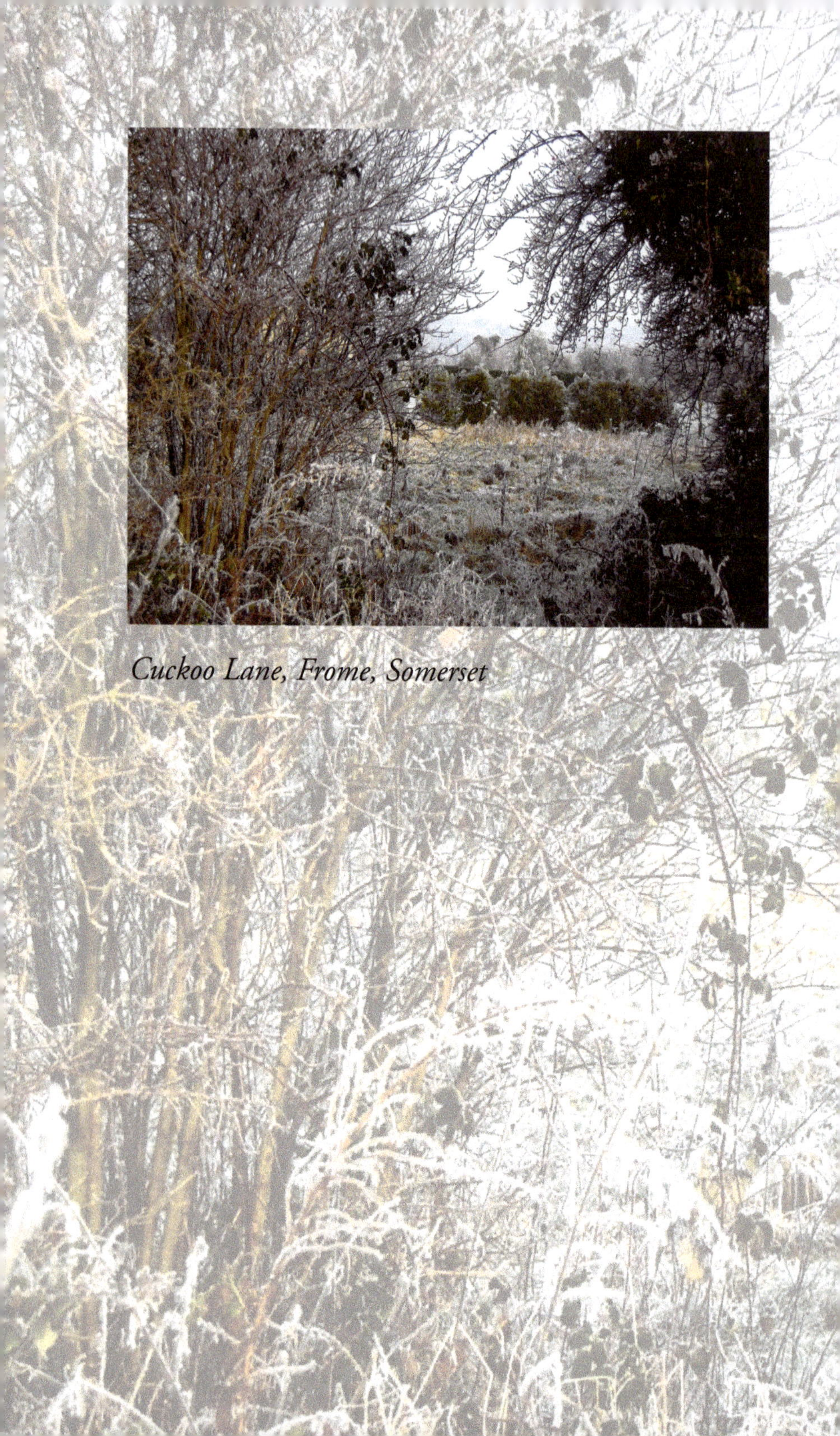

Cuckoo Lane, Frome, Somerset

22 When I Was Seventy-One

There's much to be done nearly 71,
And much more to see past 73,
Many more times I will have begun
These midwinter afternoon walks in the sun.
That wintery air still beckons me;
it allows me to ponder the heart of the tree:
older and wiser, it will continue to be
still standing long after I'm 73.

There's many mid-winters may still lie ahead,
and many more sunsets before I am dead;
there'll be much left over for others to see
long after this breath is gone from me.
And when I'm alone in that final push,
I won't hide my light under that bush;
when my winter is over, you won't catch me
longing for when I was 73.

St.Meryn, North Pembrokeshire, Wales

23 Gerontius – Part Four

Your golden age of certainty dominates your view.
The many merge as one, transparent as temporality.
Breathing your florid reason,
and boasting your faith with a knowing glance,
you find a thousand followers stamping at your gate.
Go, you participant of melody,
tuned to the simple song of the moment,
cleansed by the newness of your departure.
You are free to ride the contours in these colourful days.
They clammer as disciples at the murmuring of truth
despairing in adversity, and cowering in awe,
but all the more courageous
in the outrageous bid for your soul.
Hurry yourself through the debris of your past;
spinning round it goes, sifting your ideas and notions,
looking perhaps for God, while a fresher web is spread,
incessantly spun, distorted in the grimace
of the uneasy face of Self;
in search of a distant freedom,
deluded in the race, with no time to solve your mystery,
ever many thoughts away from the great eternal
moment.

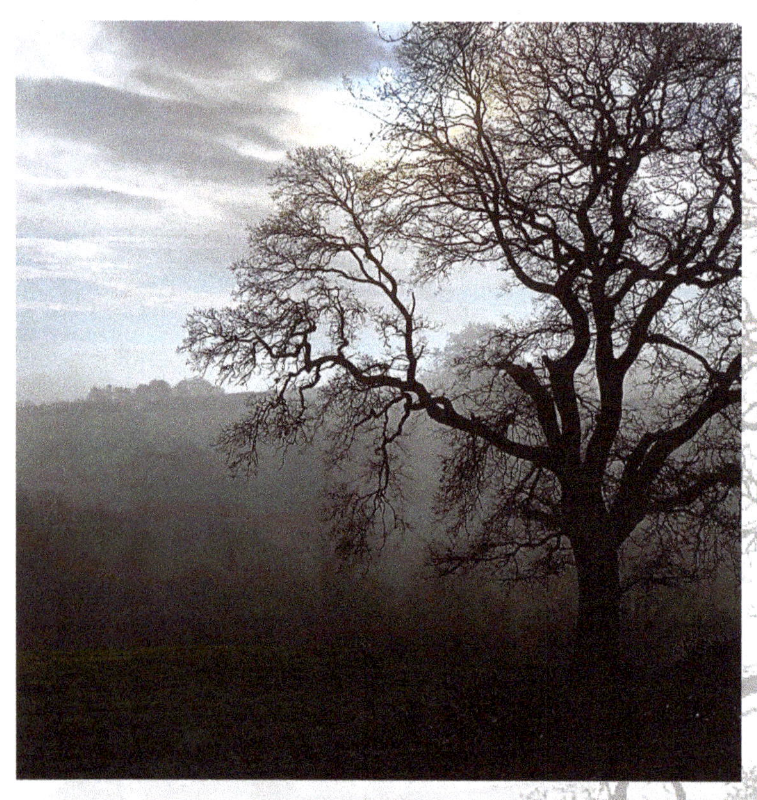

Charlcombe, Near Lansdown, Bath

24 When Darkness Falls

When darkness falls shall we yield to the night,
its blanket draped over our love?
Or shall we bid love's light still shine?
Not to allow our dream to be smothered?
A dream long since hoped for,
long since fading,
even by now, forgotten.
What steps will we tread in those shadows,
with no shaft of light, heartbeat faltering,
and direction unknown;
Will we be lost to fate and reach
for each other's hand in fear,
holding on to our forgotten faith?
Or will we harden our hearts
in the cold night air,
stiffen our lip and deny the pain,
turning away from love,
short-lived on its own gallow's tree?
Perhaps we will accept love's shortcomings,
knowing they were ours too:
shortcomings we did not see,
in the all-consuming darkness;
will we take care of love no more
and slowly watch it die?

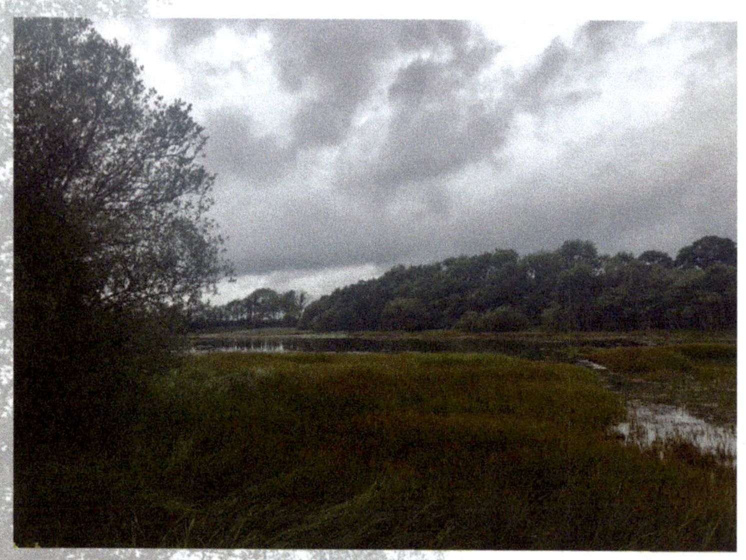

View from Pond Cottage, Landshipping, South Pembrokeshire, Wales

25 Do You Think I'm Up-Together?

Do you think I'm up-together
when I'm breezing into town?
Do you never sit like me to ask
If it's right to feel so down?
Do you really think I'm happy?
And do you then aspire
To live as though you think I do,
fulfilling my desire?
Be fair, come on, don't stick me

on this lofty pedestal.
Look between the cracks my friend,
see how the mighty fall.
I am just a shadow
of the man I used to be.
I am like a ghost afloat
upon a stagnant sea.
I am just a figment
in the eyes and ears of fools,
just another follower
of these god-forsaken rules.
So if you think I have it
all within my hands
have another look inside
to see the broken strands
of dreams and false illusions
on which I've built my life.
They're scattered in the ruins
of my pain and grief and strife.
So if you think I'm up-together
when I wander through the town?
I tell you, it's an illusion,
a façade now breaking down.

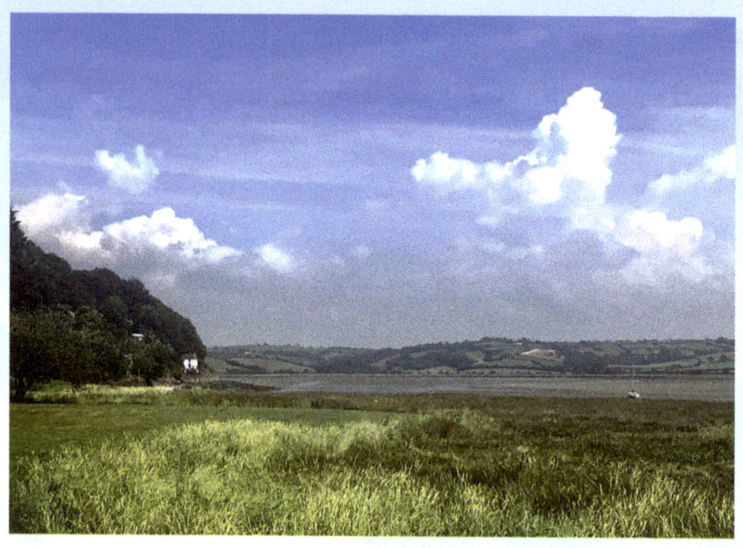

The Boat House (Dylan Thomas's Home), Laugharne, Carmarthenshire, Wales

26 Insights of Innocence

I remember the insights of innocence,
the impressionable age,
looking for a spiritual home;
the careless choice of words I'd make;
stabs in the dark at the making of a poem.
I stumble back along those paths of broken hopes,
voices deep within, that speak as a stranger
intruding upon my youth and its intimate empire.
I see a kingdom that once was mine, laid now
before me, a long-dead battleground,

all in its solitude, save for the single call of a crow,
or the far-off moans of cattle
sauntering across their oceans of meadow.
I catch myself wondering whether to fade away,
or to fly in the face of time and its ravages,
with thoughts of an inner being
never to be captured again.
I was a visitor back in the spring of time;
the seasons would soon change;
but you always stayed so close.
The warm autumn sunshine
has the warmth I used to know;
the silence in the air,
unencumbered by the roar of progress.
then flowering in the loosening of my grip.
Reaching for those strands of boyhood visions,
(illusions that coloured my world)
I stop to look upon this true earth,
the touch of nature's hand bursting
like a song beyond the senses,
invading this, my agelessness;
enduring a peace-less past,
searching till i can search no more.
Here I stand, no longer yearning
for an insight into innocence.
The passing years are calling to me....
"old man, go on.... you're already nearly home'.

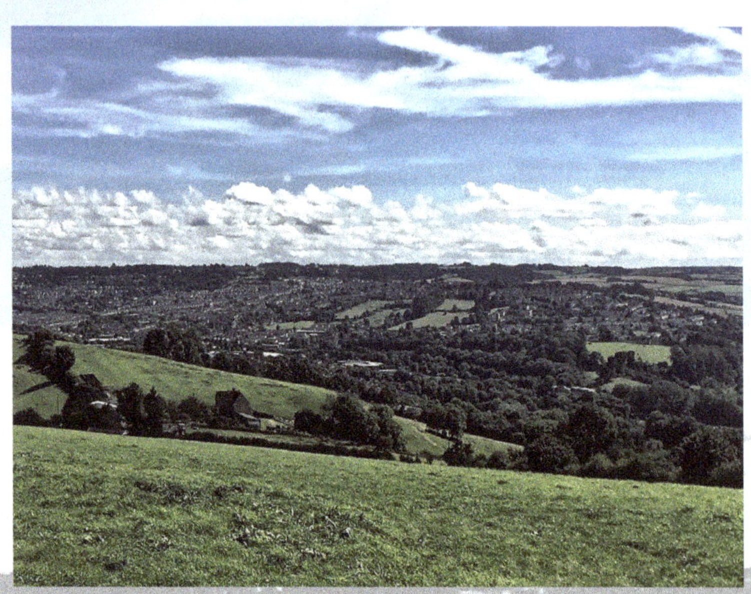

View from Lansdown over Weston, Bath

27 Wistful I

Wistful I,
not without
a yesterday smouldering,
not without
the ties as yet unjoined;
reflective, here,
musing in this
haven now provoking, I,
in retrospective dalliance
with past words

of passion coined,
contentedly sigh,
in comfort, from a dream
I'd been invoking.

If I taste
the bitter
in the poignant,
not-with-standing
the delight
of fostered memory,
I am beholden;
even tested
by the options
it's presenting,
I cannot deride
the here-to-fore,
however golden
here and now
may seem
in understanding.

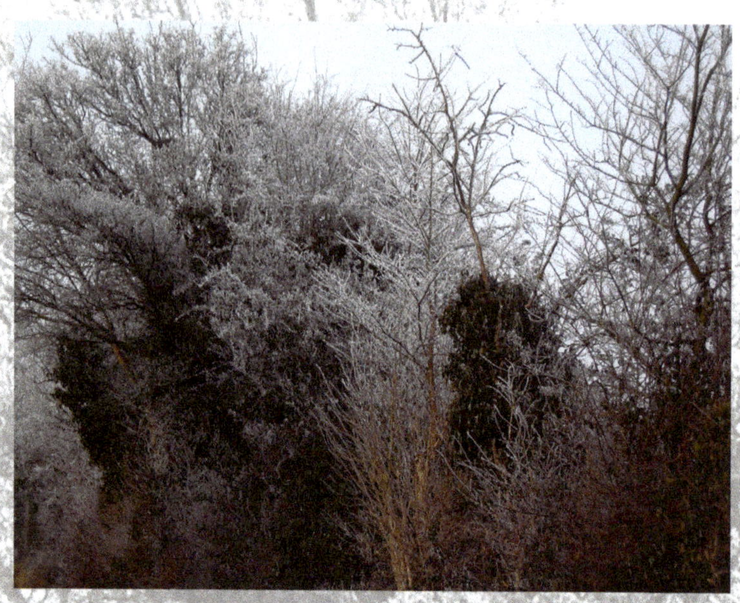

Cuckoo Lane, Frome, Somerset

28 Cast Aside by Fate

Cast aside by fate into these dark woods;
all light swallowed by shadow and dusk;
while your hungry senses
devour the far-off odour of burning leaves.
Forever looking for your home,
there's comfort in the search;
excitement in the challenge.

Tomorrow called you, even before you woke;
with plans to invade your story,

not for ambition or victory,
but to exercise your craft in the coming of the light,
and to reap its wages
as you squirm beneath its weight,
in painful anticipation
of the pain as yet to come.

For now the light is dim;
you follow a reflected moon
as she glides across your skin,
your heart now pounding; your steps a-faltering
as your legs begin to tire.
Is this the dream, or is it perhaps your butterfly,
set free from the sticky cocoon you bore
before your path was set?

All is fallng into place.
Though you are broken in mind and spirit;
and brittle in body and time,
you have stumbled here by chance.
Fate offers only vain hope
that it will heal
your historic wound.

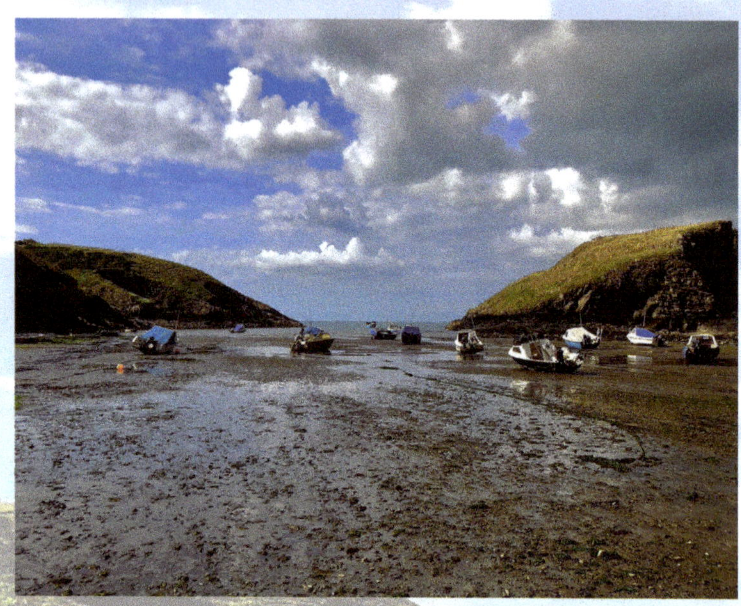

Abercastle, Pembrokeshire, Wales

29 The Winds Have Scattered the Wars of Winter

The winds have scattered the wars of winter;
your whole being strewn with the thoughts
of what could have been,
or forethought of what may be still to come.
The season's task is to allow old patterns to settle.
You watch, from here in the moment of recovery.
What was once a battleground is now your resting place.
Though once you trod over the dreams
of your brothers and sisters,

these replenished arms now carry you through,
holding you in paternal nurture;
arms like those of parents long ago
amid the weakening rays of your youthful humanity.
Recalling storms that stirred the soul,
you tread new paths at every turn.
Those bleak meanderings
left a legacy of lost opportunities
for a future lived in truth,
yet moulding your existence.
The journey moves on relentlessly
as your chances come and go,
a flickering sunlight
through a door ajar.
Watch them slip away like water
through your fingers,
and return as you loosen your grip,
too slow to catch the light.
Tortured memories of misdemeanours past
may darken your hope for survival.
You are left with aching jaws
and the sagging jowels of your age.
Chance of your salvation lingers on for another day
as you look out still holding on
to the walls of yesterday.

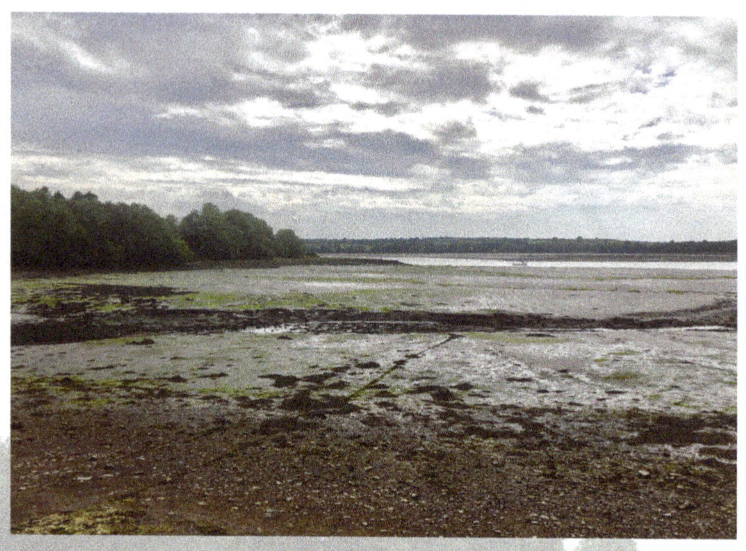

Landshipping, South Pembrokeshire, Wales

30 Gerontius – Part Five

Allow me to return to those moments long ago,
when you were heir to your own responses,
lying in beds of your own making.
Those milder moments caught you Gerontius
in an almost perfect pose.
The unfolding of your harmony was set;
through the silence the moment caught you
quivering in excited sensitivity.
The germ within you melted in the flesh;
how softly your senses did respond;

how sweet were your silences
in the face of your humanity.
You were cleansed of time and the past.
You knew nothing of your sensitivity;
and you sought no senseless fame.
You never burned for a fundamental change,
neither did you turn to confrontation,
in tune with perhaps the anger and the pain.
You knew it was not yours to gain.
Words had no soil to fall on if you spoke,
no land in which to travel
when the barriers were down.
The song you sang was not for others;
but its tune rang out as if for only them.
The world was you; and you, the song;
the song within your soul revealed that world.
And when you and the self were one,
beyond the influence of the sun,
when the end had just begun,
then your work was done.

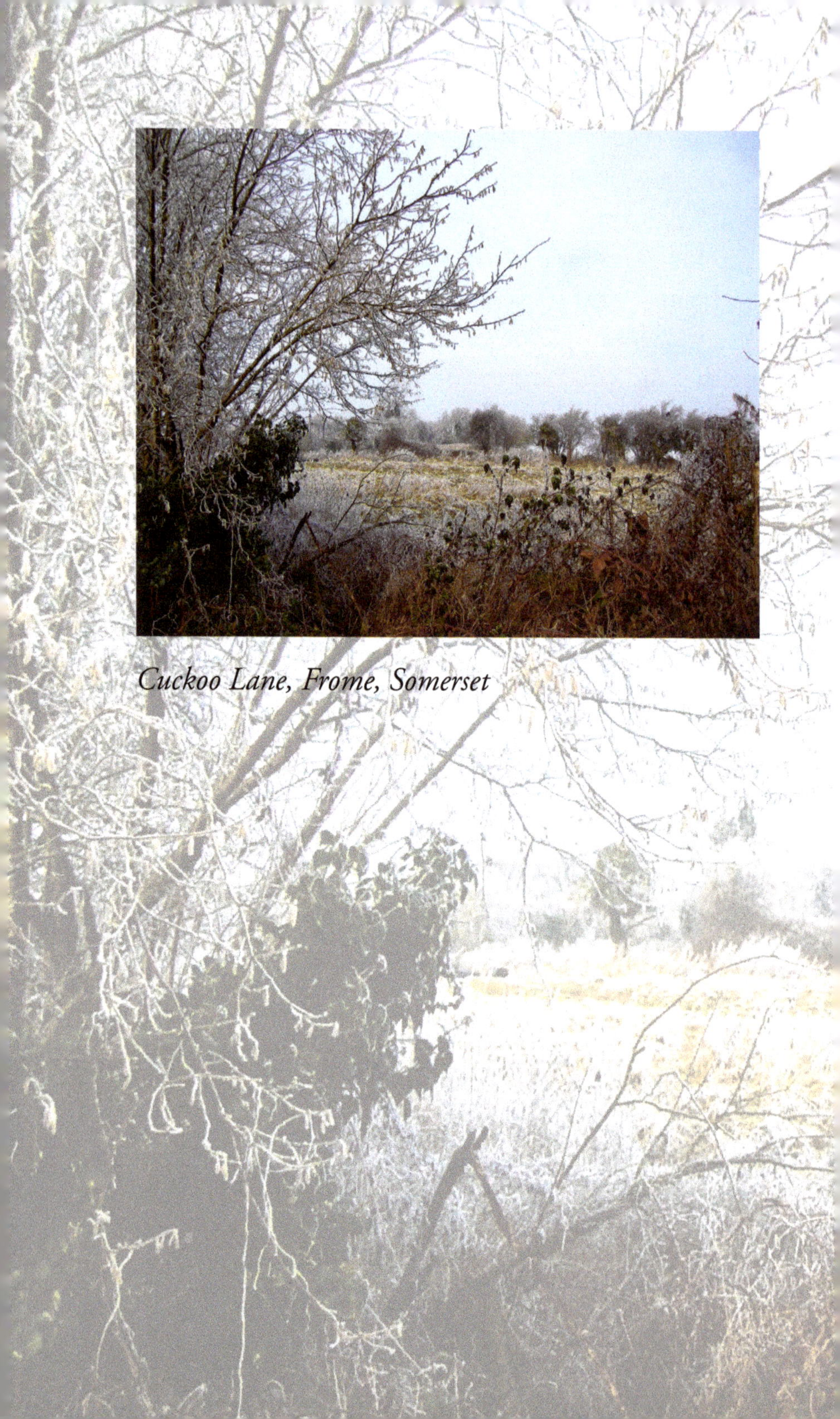

Cuckoo Lane, Frome, Somerset

31 A Quiet Passion (for Emily Dickinson)

Your life spreads – through this room –
like the scent of rosemary – on a warm spring day.
I watch tenderly – as your body drifts away.

Human frailty defined you –
You were nursemaid – to your chosen word
Born of your innocence – and inexperience.

Young and fiery then – wise –
as humility is wise –
or as an old bard – telling truths –
no pages splashed – no bursts of emotion.

Modesty rang – from your torture –
confident self-assertion –
not swallowed up – by regret.

Forlorn – you convulsed into death –
words and phrases – reflect your quiet passion –
epitome of epiphanies.

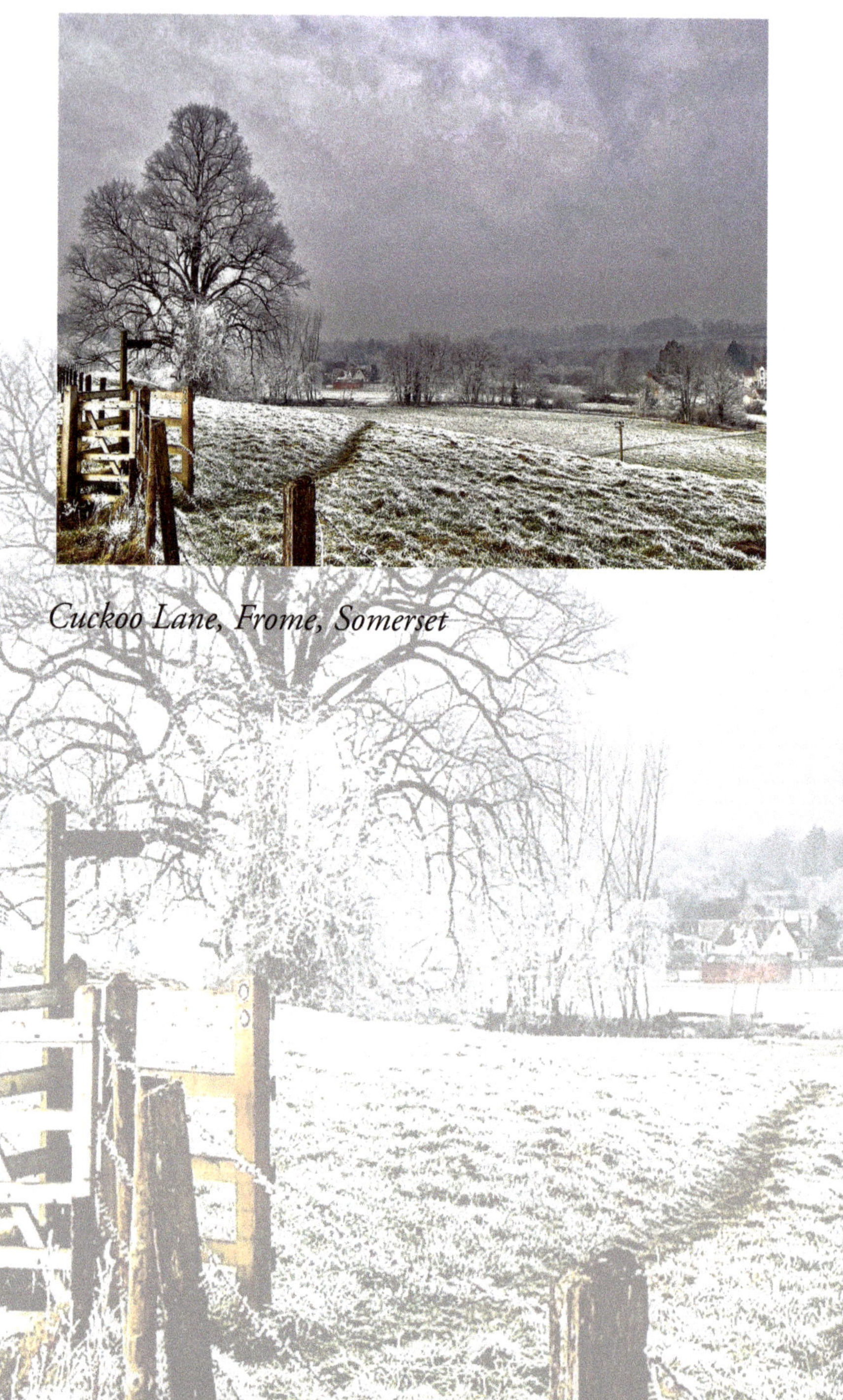

Cuckoo Lane, Frome, Somerset

32 Hearts Remain Loveless

The greenest rivers flow by here;
the earth is fresh and dark brown,
the healthy soil of a new found land
untouched by lust or craving for more,
and moistened at the river's edge.
Rivers that carry away all debris
and deposit the silt they reap.
Just as the soil is wet,
so do the shoots show face;
the reeds sing their notes
never pausing for breath,
nor stirring too quick,
nor bending too far
in the watery breeze.
Though the land is bright,
the birds have left their trees
to gather by the banks;
and hearts remain loveless,
watching for night to fall.

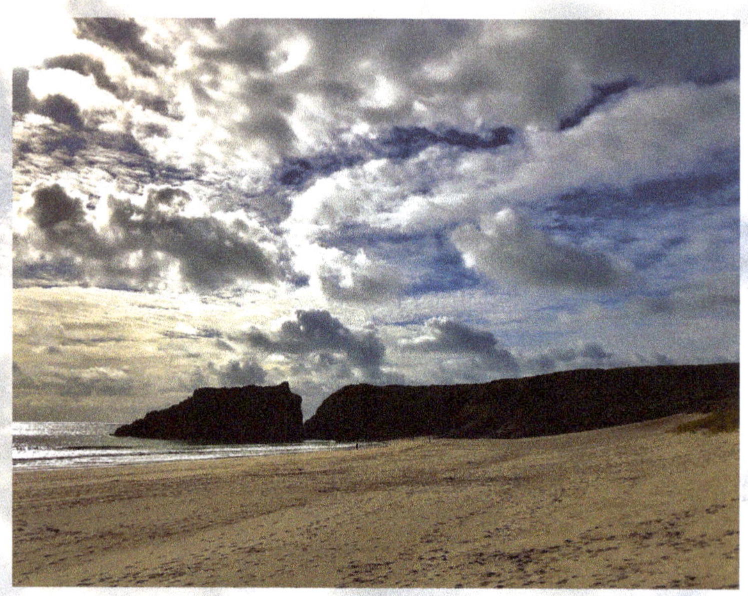

Broadwater, South Pembrokeshire, Wales

33 Gerontius – Part Six

Those who live on, on this sacred journey,
and tamper with its essence,
taunting the seasons with wild experimentation,
if they dare the soul disrupt compassion,
they will burn out the cells of their reason,
leaving them naked in the chains of their being,
weeping for the dead, or choking
on so many half-forgotten truths.
They cannot comprehend their sense's infertility.
In death, their innocence extinguished,

the fires of their lives now doused,
they will stand in all their justification,
accounting for their existence,
expounding the knowledge they had gained,
blinded by simplicity, and unable to survive
in the blandness of their vacuum; there,
in the never perfect silence, with the babble of
vocabulary,
and the noise of their descriptions,
now sediment in the nectar of death's reality.
They campaigned for a glimpse of death in their
religions,
but the dying took place while their backs turned,
when their thoughts were at war with their past.
But ah! The curtain of death is raised to reveal
a light that's never shone in thought;
a light that moistens the arid pastures of grief,
pity in the soul that self-sacrifice could never had
known.
They dissolve in the touch of your glorious revelation.
These impatient mortals weep fond farewells,
contaminating the consummation of mortality:
life and death separated by man's sorrow.

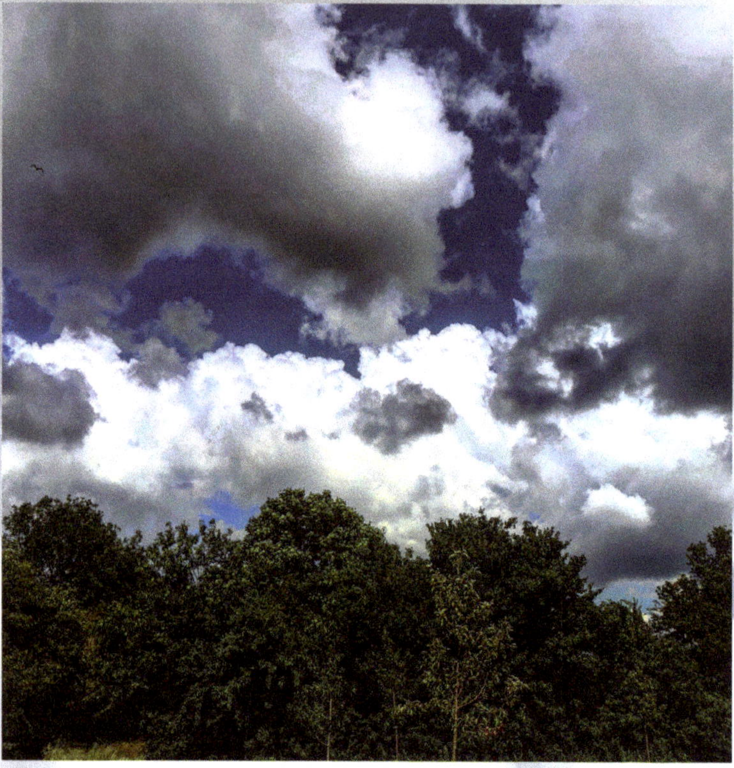

Clouds and Treetops with Blue Sky, Berkley, Near Frome, Somerset

34 Unsolicited Life

It's all vaguely familiar,
here in the hinterland,
lost regions of so many endings,
the edge of this world I call my life.
Seems I walked this way before;
imagined or might have dreamed
on nights I'd have rather deleted,
having depleted all my power.
There's no-one here but me,
and so I gather sticks
ready to live life to completion;
this unsolicited life.

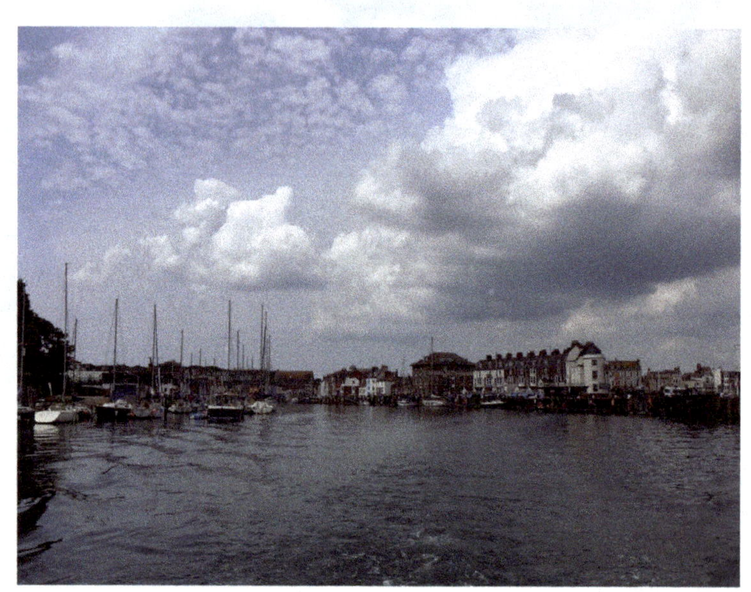

Weymouth, Dorset

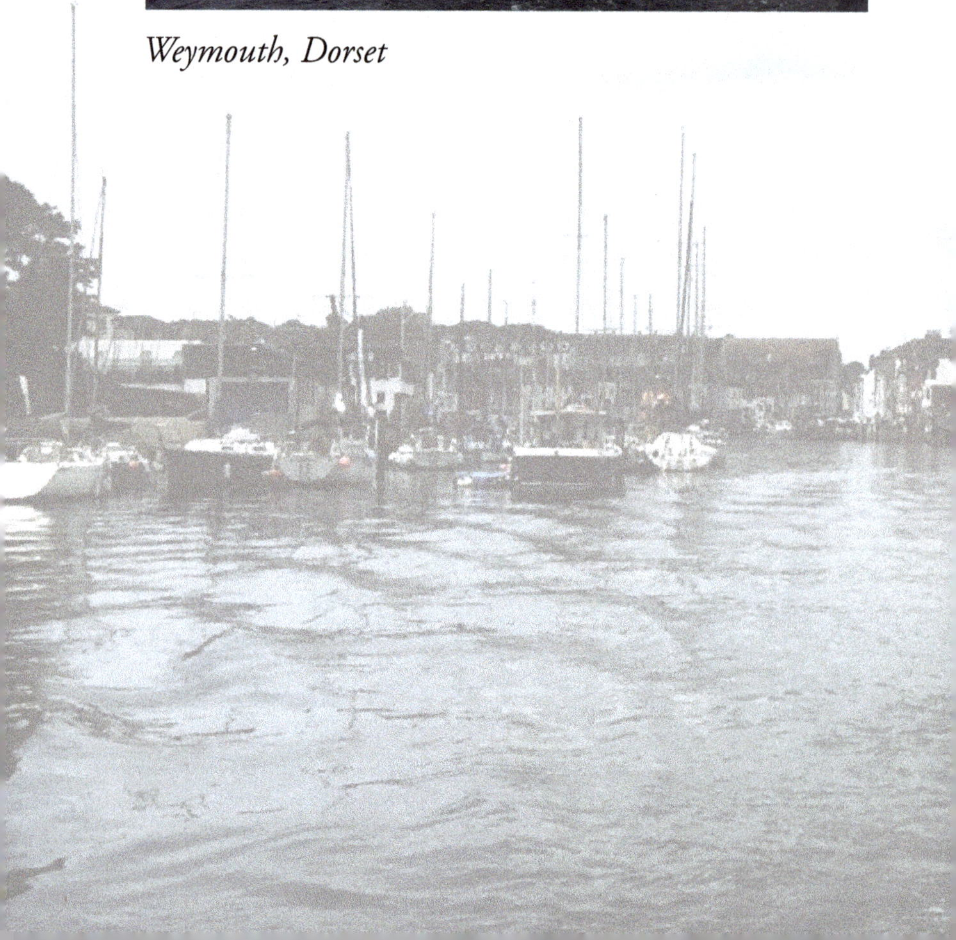

35 Summer, the Apex of Seasons

Burst forth, buckled by the sun,
wondrous world complete,
this, the apex of seasons,
full of life in swollen buds,
caressed by the sensuous,
loved in the moment.

Majestic blossom stood aside,
in spontaneous expression
through senses unsensing,
feelings unfeeling, human to earth,
each touch, each world
exploding in unforgotten bliss.

Thought disturbs the peace;
memory floods the now;
no stone unturned.
But yearnings for a clearer dawn;
avoiding the sultry present
that claims to be the truth,
as it hides in in the undergrowth
away from the summer's height.

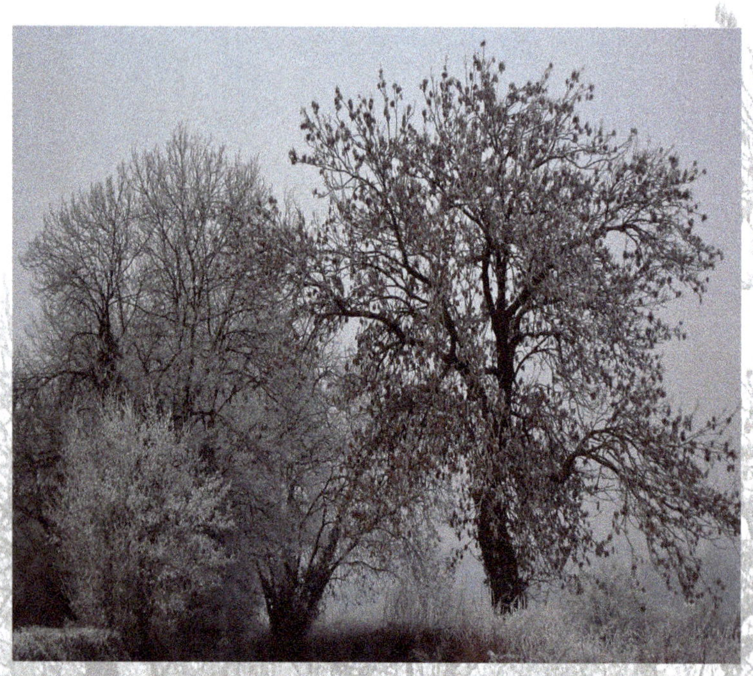

Cuckoo Lane, Frome Somerset

36 Mercifully Open to Reason

Mercifully open to reason, you,
not too tough for a sensitive heart,
not too cold for a shivering child,
let him reach for my hand to hold,
this child in his solitude,
unprotected from those who question.

And if reason depletes his soul,
or disturbs his innocence,
let mercy open his heart,
to bleed into nature's crevices,
where all thought dissolves,
and the child remains equal
to all who would question
his innocent right to be free.

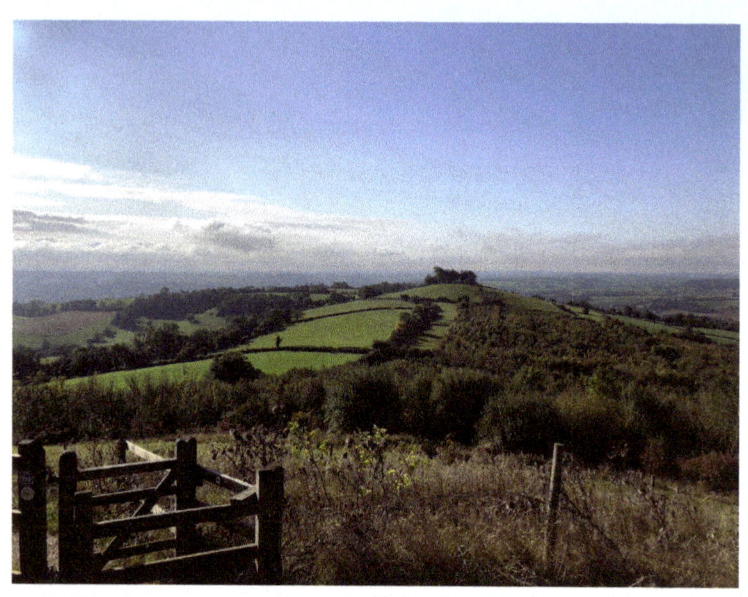

From Lansdown Racecourse looking South, Near Bath

37 I Sat in a Blazing Heat

I sat in a blazing heat
watching them all pass by;
shimmering silhouettes,
with faces in the haze wearing
all the hopelessness of the age.
These souls broke into my thoughts long past,
trampling through my contemplation,
my gentle respite from a world I cannot love.

I can feel the remnants of my old blank face;
lost to a cold existence, my soul drained of hope.
I gaze through the rays of an unforgiving sun,
and nurture my long-since child.
All distant and detached, and reckless as a butterfly,
my words come spilling out,
burning the sun-drenched ground at my feet.

Though my voice stays quiet
my heart still sings,
lost causes all abandoned;
hidden all this time and more,
nothing forced,
all awry, done forever.
I weep no more for tomorrow,
one hand held by a beckoning child,
the other tugging my arm,
returning me home
to the heaven I found hope in:
this room where I was born;
this canny place
where the sins of the fathers
are no longer cleansed
by the achievements of their sons.

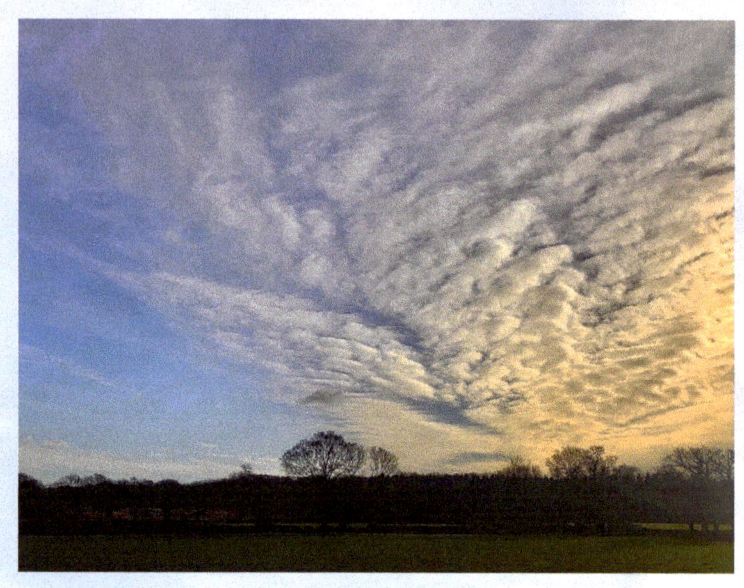

Charlcombe, Near Lansdown, Bath

38 The Quietness of Death (for John Hills)

Let him enter where silence now prevails;
silence will caress
where flesh and idle thought dissolve,
knowing only this:
ideas were but embellishment,
while truth lives on
beyond the words we use.
Let him float in the quietness of death
void of sound, clear of mind.
This will be a space
where the dangers disperse,
and the ravages of life
have lost their power.
Then leave him there in peace at last,
with the clean air
and a gentle breeze.

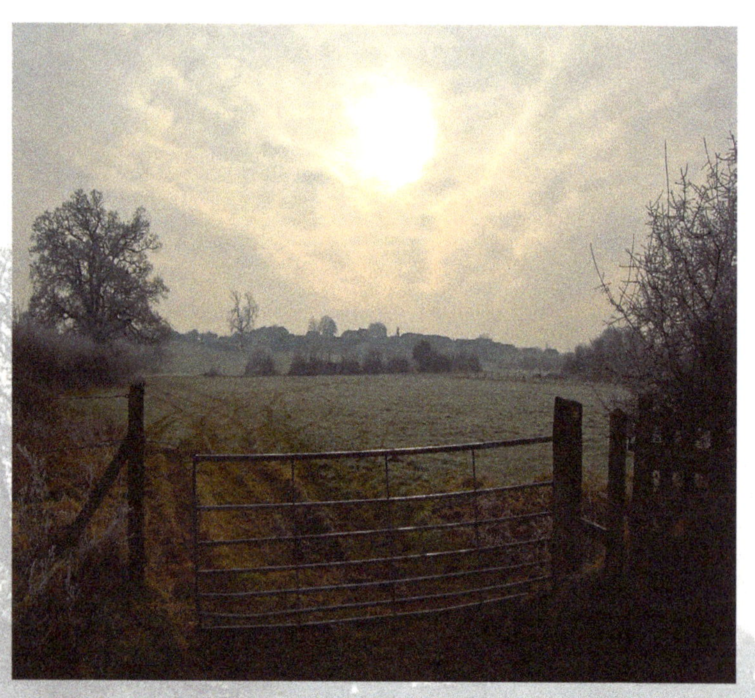

View from Standerwick towards Berkley, Near Frome, Somerset

39 Costas – Friend in My Youth and of My Youth

Blood on blood,
friend in my youth and of my youth,
your ashes I taste upon my lips.
I remember your square hips,
leather jacket
and bleached blue jeans.
You were my angular friend,
unafraid to stand alone.
It took years for me to be so strong.
You moved so swiftly.
turning around
to beckon me on,
you, riding the crest of waves
that would swallow me up;
me, floundering in the wash,
knowing all along
I would survive you.

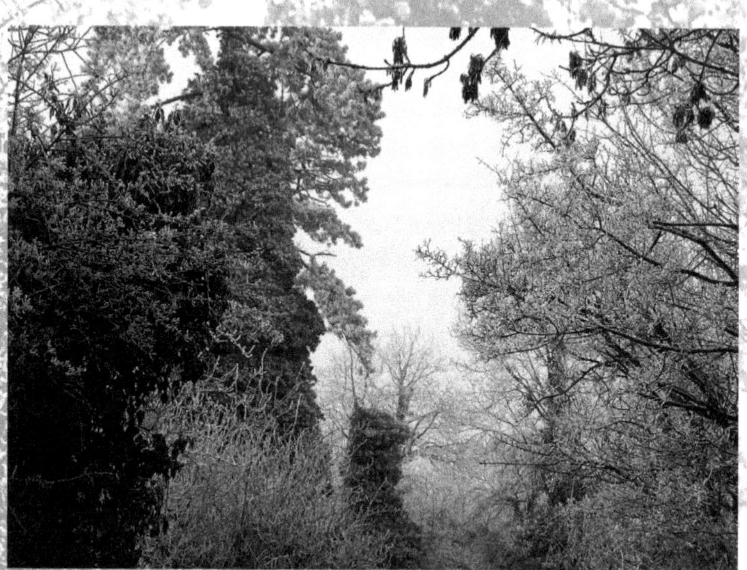

Cuckoo Lane, Frome, Somerset

40 Gerontius – Part Seven

New life within your grasp
opens up your pores;
the water absorbed in the flowers.
To you, Gerontius, they cannot lie;
to you my dove, so close to home,
so much a part of your own divinity;

they will not lie, nor even try.
New life lingers around your senses;
you break through
like a winter sun through cloud,
illuminate the vision, you the traveller;
your journey is to places never known;
they will respond to your sensibility,
and live within
the opening of your Spring;
they were born
before the season was fragile;
be gentle with your senses as they sing.
There's a strange silence
in your black ceremony.
Without thinking,
you set your speculation free.
You float in irresistible fortune, like me,
released in the fertile streams
that saturate your soil.
Your essence breathes,
lives on beyond this ritual of death,
though your sacrifice be torment
to the sorrowful,
disturbing the foundations
of their cultured satisfactions.
This is your living testimonial,
the laying down of dignity
in the making of your soul.

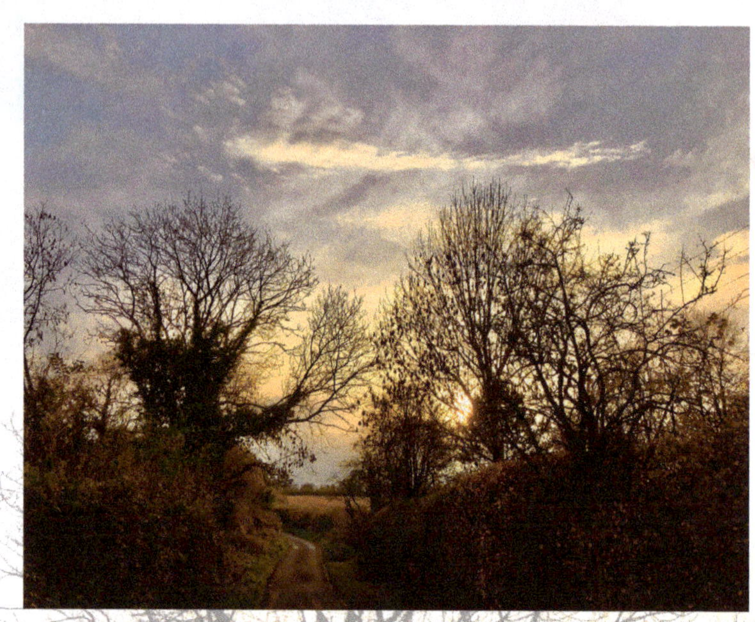

Cuckoo Lane, Frome, Somerset

41 Cley Hill

I walked late Autumn, Cley Hill way.
Greens and browns and hazy grey.
The wind bit hard, but the heart was warm.
Welcome to the gates of Winter.

The earth was hard, then it was soft;
the grass was wet, leaning to the east.
I followed my heart unafraid,
free from the lands below.

High above the ground, high above myself,
the paths fell under my feet so easily;
the wind around my head
tousled my hair, and the shrubs and the hedge.

The voice of the wind bid its own welcome
and my heart burst forth with the joy of sight.

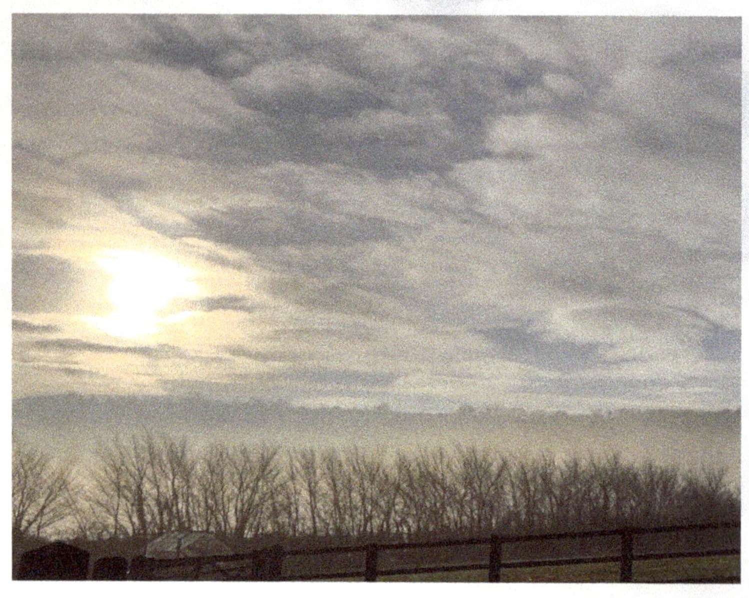

Charlcombe, Near Lansdown, Bath

42 Autumn Rushes In

Autumn rushes in,
summer wanders out.
I've been here before;
there isn't any doubt.
You can see me now
as I always was,
sitting in my den,
happier because...

Autumn rushes in,
summer wanders out.
My heart begins to soar;
my voice no more to shout.
For this is how I am
and as I always was,
once a raging lion,
milder now because...

Autumn rushes in,
summer wanders out.
The taste is on my tongue;
the bonfire smoke's about.
I can hear the clock
ticking like it does;
counting through the day;
softer now, because...

Autumn rushes in,
summer wanders out.
Leaves begin to fall;
there isn't any doubt.

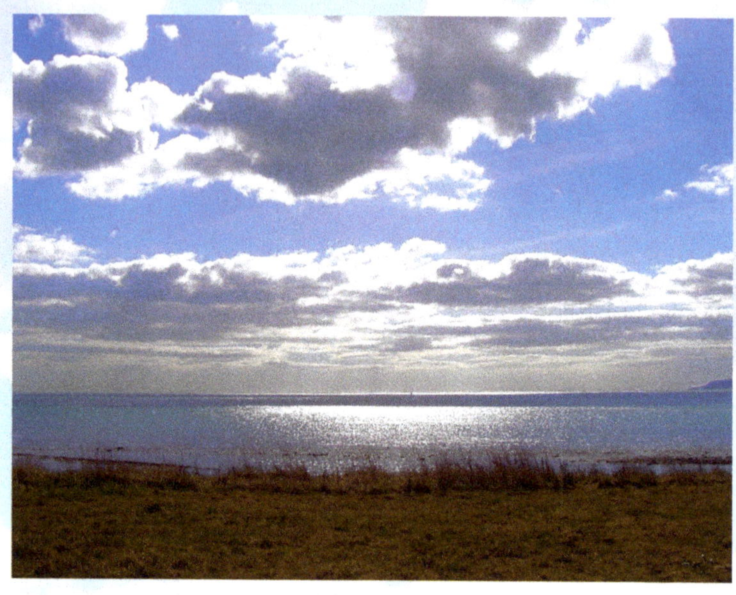

Ringstead, Dorset

43 Dream Heaven, Formed of Your Wish

(For Katie and Lizzi aged 9 and 7)

You two,
out of whose heaven,
rain falls;
flowers;
drops of your
ever to be
petal-love of mine;
petals dropping;
rain,

again, again.
My children;
blood of mine,
whispering blood of mine,
flowering buds of child,
how shall I speak to you?
I speak to you but voice,
but moments past,
but sound.
How shall I measure
that which I do not touch,
which I do not see?
Burden though this is,
you are no weight.
Perfect though I seem,
I am yet to be seen.
I am green,
I am moribund,
I am child,
unknowing of you,
of them, off-spring,
either of those loves.
I am master
of the torrid scene,
not to be seen,
only to seem,
and be green to you
even though
you are no weight.

Only to be lost,
father to you
only in word;
not heard;
word not heard.
Oh child, bird,
fly away
to a distant land,
but never leave
my gentle hand for you,
outstretched in wild
and lost hope,
mercy begging;
rugged hand
still soft in palm
and longing
to be touched.
Take a book,
or diamonds thrust,
or any thus such token
love demands;
but take, young pair,
a leaf of my
lost soul for you;
the part I carry
deep within a father's tomb;
a part wherein
a world is formed;
a lost world

your young eyes remember,
to be found on distant days,
full and avid,
fine and blue,
and made for you,
and me.
Be still in sleep,
but dream heaven
formed of your wish;
child, children,
wish for me
as I will always
wish for you.
But live!
And give to others, true;
and live in others,
I for you;
live, you two,
for others,
please my darlings, live!
I do, for you.

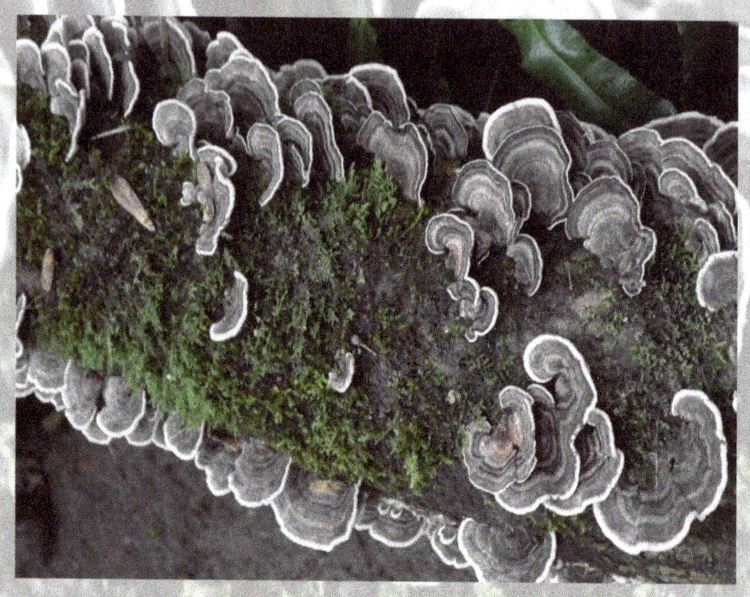

A favourite log by the stream – Nunney, Near Frome, Somerset

44 A Part of Me

A part of me asks
a tantalising start.
Tasks I partake in,
I make a mistake in;
a part of me asks
an incredible part.
But "I am whole",
answers my soul;
though my soul it is dim,
unaware that within
is a wonderful part;
just a part;
only some.
I am long-suffering;
I am whole;
but in part
just a little numb.

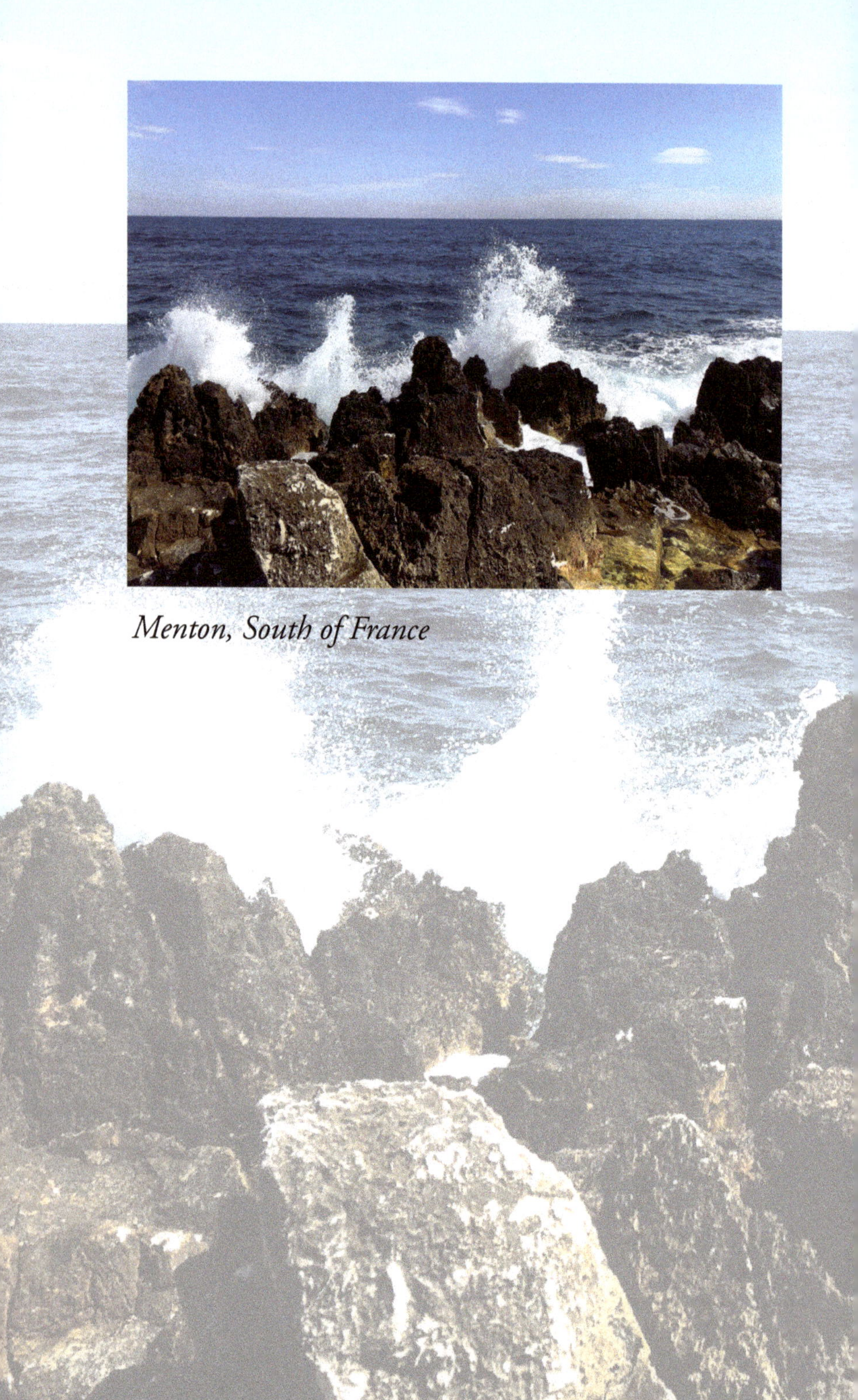

Menton, South of France

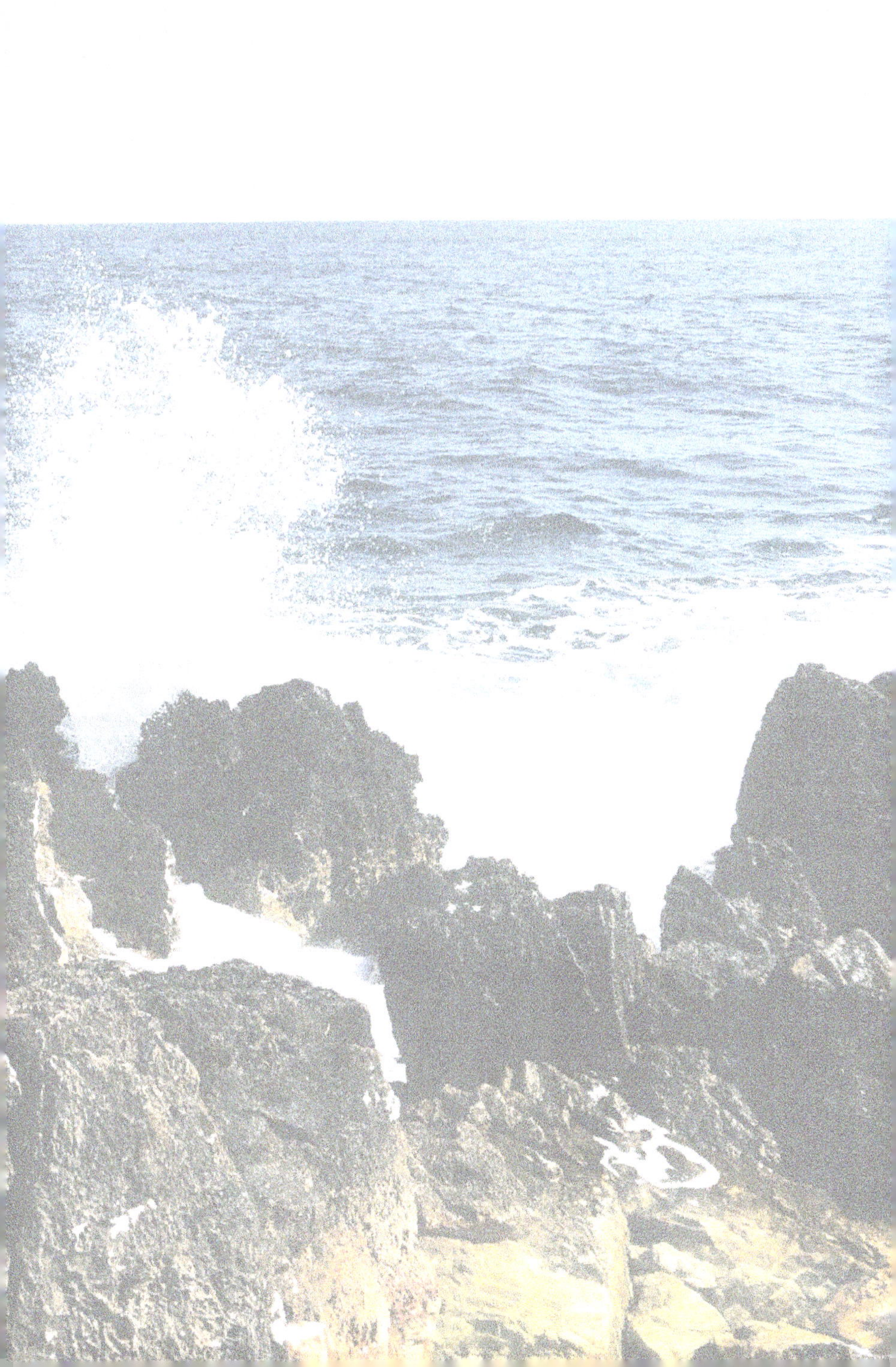

www.ingramcontent.com/pod-product-compliance
Lightning Source LLC
LaVergne TN
LVHW052354100826
845147LV00013B/843

* 9 7 8 1 9 1 4 4 0 7 3 1 4 *